new
trends
in
commercial
spaces

Office for Metropolitan Architecture
Arad Associated Fabio Novembre
Partners Renzo Piano Building Wo
Antonio Citterio & Partners Ph
& R. Riley Venturi, Scott Bro
Architetti Diller + Sc
(S.Cottrell, J.Michela
Alexander McQu
Office dA Juha
Gorgona Bo
Rune Mic
D'Ambro
Thoma
Arc
Ma
& I
Arc
Par

(OMA) Architecture Studio Ron
Jun Aoki + Eric Carlson Gehry
kshop Eduardo Souto de Moura
ipe Starck Bohlin Cywinski Jackson
vn & Associates Lazzarini Pickering
idio Jean Nouvel IAD arquitectos
geli) Antonello Boschi John Pawson
een + William Russell Steven Holl
llonen 3deluxe Jakob+MacFarlane
hm Associates Claesson, Koivisto &
ael Young Rei Kawakubo Giovanni
io NL Architects for Droog Design
Schlesser 6a architects BOX
itectes Michael Gabellini Thom
ne - Morphosis Kauffmann Theilig
artner Propeller Z Neil M. Denari
itects, Inc. Sergio Calatroni
nership Ernst Beneder Ian Hay

new trends *in* commercial *spaces*
Work concept: Carles Broto
Publisher: Arian Mostaedi

Graphic design & production: Pilar Chueca

Text: Contributed by the architects, edited
      by Jacobo Krauel and Amber Ockrassa

© Carles Broto i Comerma
Jonqueres, 10, 1-5
08003 Barcelona, Spain
Tel.: +34 93 301 21 99 Fax: +34-93-301 00 21
E-mail: info@linksbooks.net
www. linksbooks.net

ISBN: 84-96263-30-4

Printed in China
Edition 2005

new trends in commercial spaces

structure

Introduction

There are trend setters and there are trend followers. Trend setters rewrite the old rules that trend followers then obey. It is the trend setters that we were looking for in putting together this collection. We were looking for new interpretations, fresh viewpoints, innovations. In short, we were looking for designs that are destined to determine the future of architecture. The results of our search are varied. In order to give a representative vision of the most innovative creations of recent years, we have tried as far as possible to show the great diversity of commercial spaces and their almost infinite decorative possibilities in order to provide a grpahic guide to current and future tendencies in the design of interiors for attention to the public.

Fashion shops, the sector that is most dependent on the added value of the brand in the choice of the product, are particularly susceptible to differentation through design. They thus offer visual characteristics that immediately identify the brand of clothes that they offer, even suggesting the scenarios -whether exotic, elegant or down-to-earth- for the lifestyle that is associated with their garments.

Since technical know-how is just as important as artistic vision in any project, we have touched upon every aspect in the design and construction processes to give a well-rounded vision.

From conception to completion, we have included information on material and construction processes in order to complement the design ideas of the contributing architects. Finally, since nobody is in a better position to comment on these projects than the designers themselves, we have included the architects' own comments and anecdotes.

Therefore, we trust that we are leaving you in good, expert hands and that this selection of some of the finest, most innovative architectural solutions in the world will serve as an endless source of inspiration. Enjoy!

Office for Metropolitan Architecture (OMA)
Prada New York Epicenter

New York City, USA

Prada's latest New York project is an interior conversion of the former Guggenheim store in Soho. The 23,000 square feet are distributed between the ground floor and basement of the building. A translucent wall of polycarbonate covers the existing brick wall of the building and establishes a dialogue between old and new. A mural of wallpaper on the entire length of the store allows for rapid change of the environment.

As a means to naturally connect to the basement and guide customers to the more invisible parts of the store, the floor steps downwards in its entire width and rises subsequently to re-connect to the ground level, creating a big 'wave'.

Located at the Broadway entrance, a round and fully glazed elevator displays bags and accessories. It descends into a lounge located underneath the wave, where the main dressing rooms are visible from display mattresses covered in techno gel that enable visitors to sit and watch people dress. The black-and-white marble floor is a reference to the first Prada store in Milan. The northern part of the basement holds the archive, which is composed of 'movable walls', an adapted system of compact shelving that allows the sequence and size of spaces to be altered according to need. These Prada-green shelves contrast with the unfinished gypsum board walls and the wooden ceiling.

A series of experiential and service-oriented features enhances both the functioning and the ambience of the stores. The dressing rooms are equipped with 'magic mirrors': a plasma screen invisibly built into the large mirror surface that allows customers to see themselves both from the front and the back at the same time. An integrated time delay can even capture and replay movements.

The doors are made of Privalite glass that the customer can switch from transparent to translucent to control the privacy of the dressing room. Equipped with RFID [radio frequency identity] antennas, the 'garment closet' is able to register merchandise brought into the dressing room and display an inventory of icons on a touch screen. Here, the customer can request more specific information on the clothes, but also browse through alternative items of the collection.

Photographs: Armin Linke, OMA & Prada

Site plan

Ramp sections

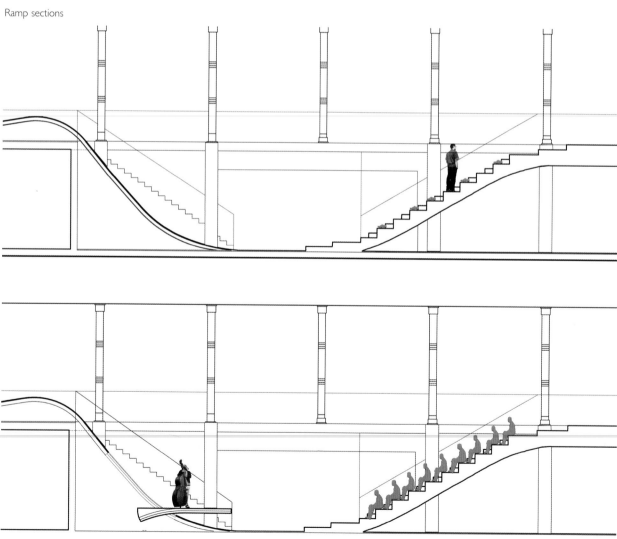

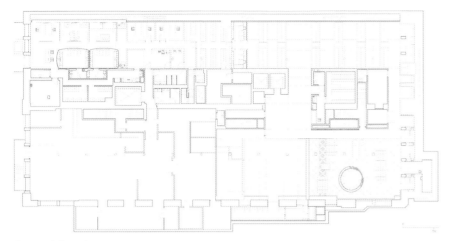

Basement floor plan

As a means to naturally connect to the basement and guide customers to the more invisible parts of the store, the floor steps downwards in its entire width and rises subsequently to re-connect to the ground level, creating a big 'wave'. The oversized stair made of zebra wood is used as an informal display space. At the push of a button, an event platform rotates out of the opposite part of the wave, turning the stair into an auditorium for performances, film projections and lectures.

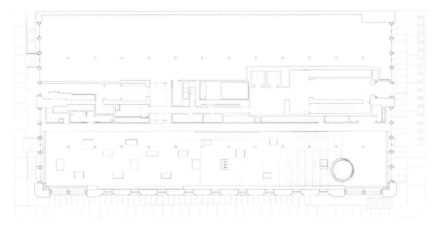

Ground floor plan

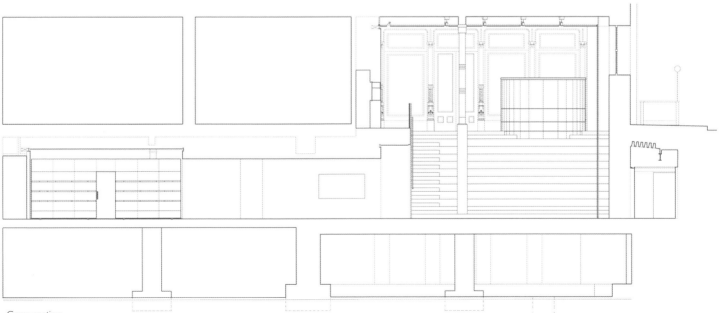

Cross section

13

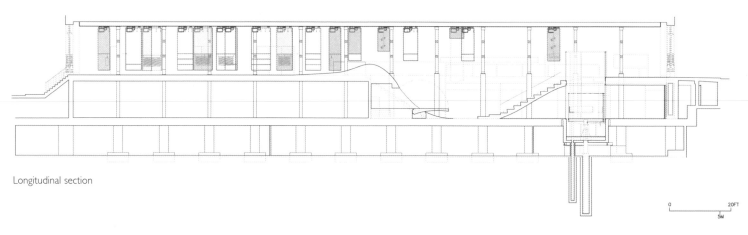

Longitudinal section

0   20FT
5M

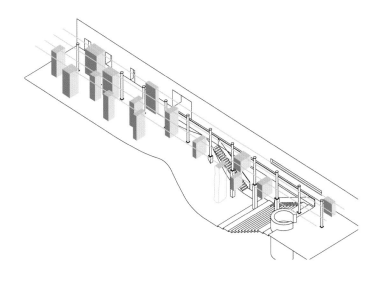

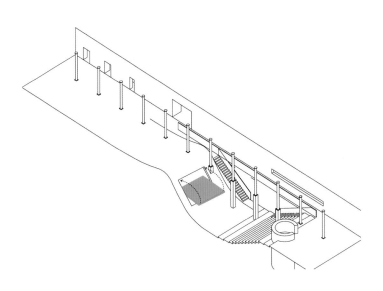

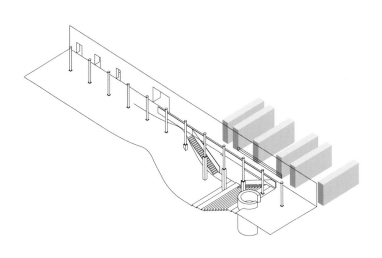

Renzo Piano Building Workshop
Maison Hermès

Tokyo, Japan

The French Group Hermès chose a 6000 m² building in Tokyo's Ginza district for its Japanese headquarters. This project was both aesthetically and technically challenging. How, in the architectural diversity of Tokyo, could a "landmark" building be conceived, one that would also comply with Japan's strict earthquake standards?

The idea of a "magic lantern" like those hung in the doors of Japanese houses soon arose; a facade made entirely from 45x45 cm glass blocks successfully imparts this aspect of the design.

The innovative anti-seismic system was inspired by traditional Japanese temples that are still standing despite frequent earthqakes. The backbone of this building is made up of a flexible steel structure that is articulated at structurally strategic locations with visco-elastic dampers, from which cantilevered floors extend to support the suspended glass-block facades.

The entire building can move during earthquakes, thanks to predefined displacements, uniformly distributed throughout the structure.

A small, open square at the center connects the street to the subway station via a long escalator. A mobile sculpture by the artist Susumu Shingu overlooks this space from atop the building.

Photographs: Michel Denancé

The floor plan of this 15-floor-building measures 45x11 meters. As a response to Japan's strict seismic controls, the backbone of the building is made up of a flexible steel structure that is articulated at structurally strategic points with visco-elastic dampers, from which cantilevered floors extend to support the suspended glass-block facades.

Ground floor plan

Second floor plan

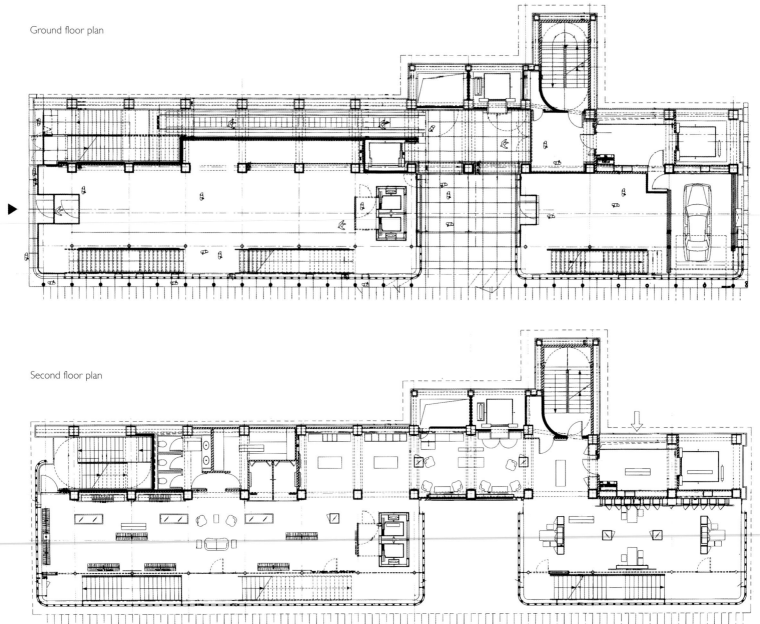

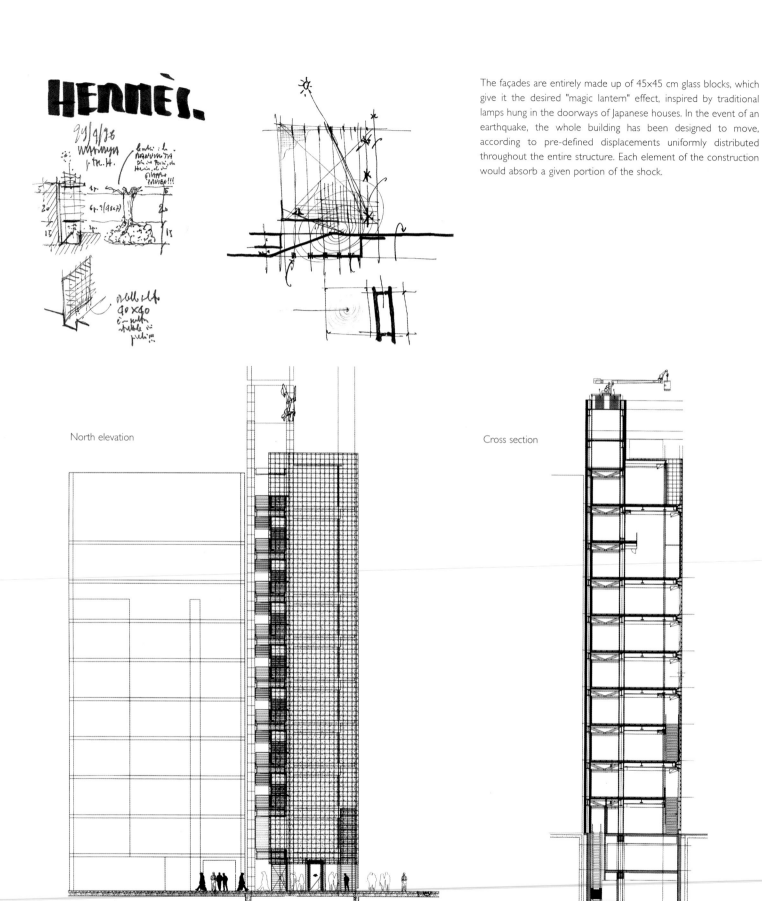

The façades are entirely made up of 45×45 cm glass blocks, which give it the desired "magic lantern" effect, inspired by traditional lamps hung in the doorways of Japanese houses. In the event of an earthquake, the whole building has been designed to move, according to pre-defined displacements uniformly distributed throughout the entire structure. Each element of the construction would absorb a given portion of the shock.

North elevation

Cross section

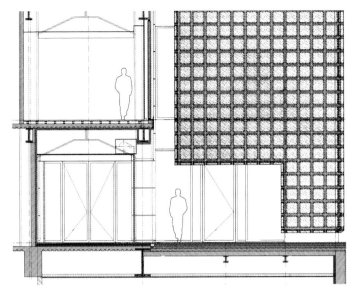

Eduardo Souto de Moura
Clérigos Art Gallery

Oporto, Portugal

The basic structure of the Clérigos Art Gallery by the Portuguese architect Eduardo Souto de Moura is identical to that of the shop that was previously located on this site. Only a wall has been added to separate the public part of the premises from the area used by the employees.

The wall on which the works of art will be placed thus becomes a fundamental element of the scheme. It consists of a steel structure supported at two points, filled with Ytong and plastered with ochre-colored sand from Barcelos. The premises are generously illuminated by the large glazed openings that form the facade of the gallery and in turn allow the works of art to be seen from the outside.

Today there is a common idea, not shared by this architect, that spaces for exhibiting works of art must be neutral, without elements that distract the attention from the objects on display - as if Klee´s angles could not be placed inside a baroque church.

Photographs: Luís Ferreira Alves

Floor plan

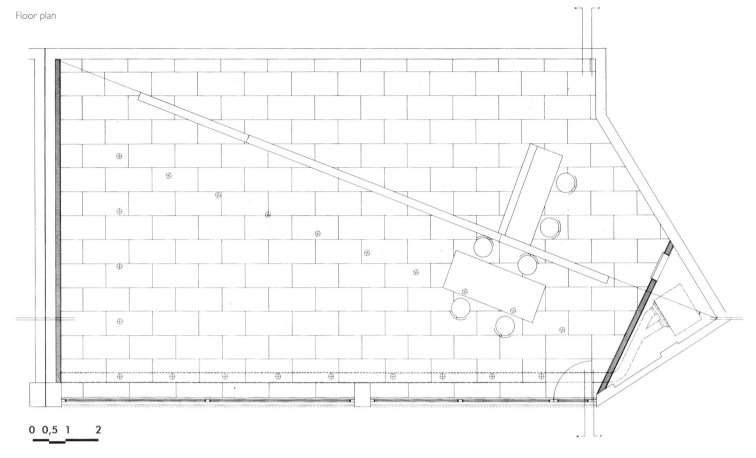

0 0,5 1   2

Longitudinal sections

A large opening allows light to enter the gallery, illuminating the wall on which the works of art will be hung. The wall was plastered with ochre-colored sand from Barcelos.

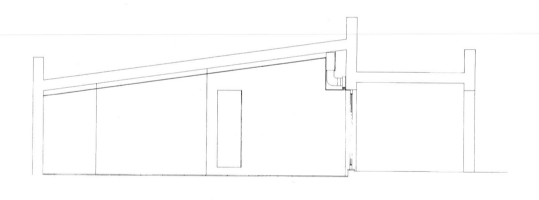

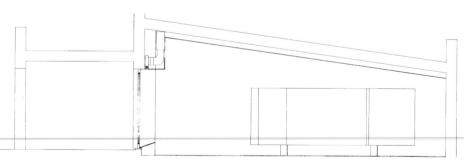

Cross sections

Antonio Citterio & Partners
B&B store

Milan, Italy

The new B&B store in Milan enjoys a privileged location in a land-mark 1960's building and occupies a total floor space, with ground level and basement, of 1700 m². The design for the shop includes spectacular, open-plan double height volumes on the ground level and various openings leading toward the basement. Throughout the space are the results of experimentation with transparent glass volumes contrasted against opaque masses.

The Maxalto Collection is presented within a massive black rectangular MDF volume, which is suspended on thin columns and is cantilevered toward the façade. Green and yellow glass boxes break up the ground floor space and serve as ideal spaces for displaying individual pieces.

At the back of the space is a mezzanine housing the offices, which are partially shielded from public view by semi-reflecting gray glass panels. Inside are a kitchen, custom-designed by Antonio Citterio, and bathroom, also from Citterio's collection. All materials have been selected with the intention of creating a dramatic interplay of contrasting elements. The floor is composed of an elegantly polished black iron-oxide cement, which is dramatically set off by cream-colored walls that were treated by soaking gauze in the freshly painted surface. The thickness of the brightly colored glass of the display cases is shown off by leaving the edges unframed. The broad staircase leading to the basement level is done in an acid treated steel, while the low walls surrounding it are composed of double sheets of acid-etched glass. In general, neutral shades and backgrounds lacking strength of character were rigorously avoided.

Photographs: Fabrizio Bergamo

Basement floor plan

0 1 5m

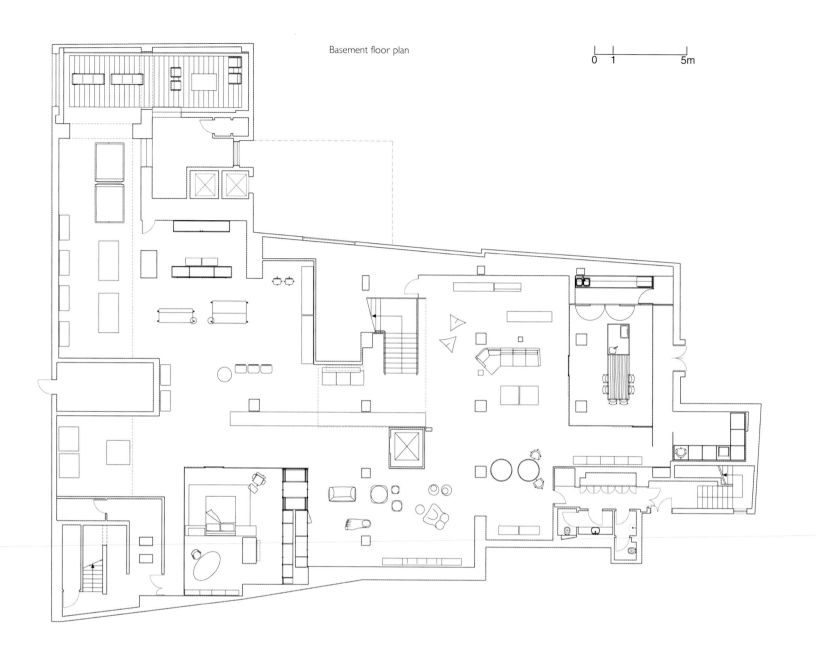

Longitudinal section

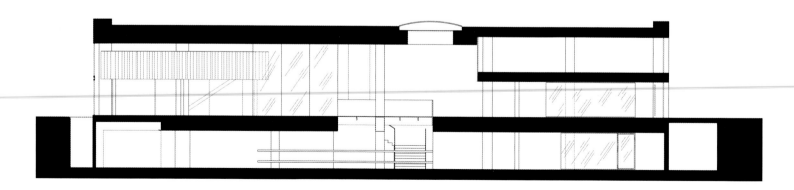

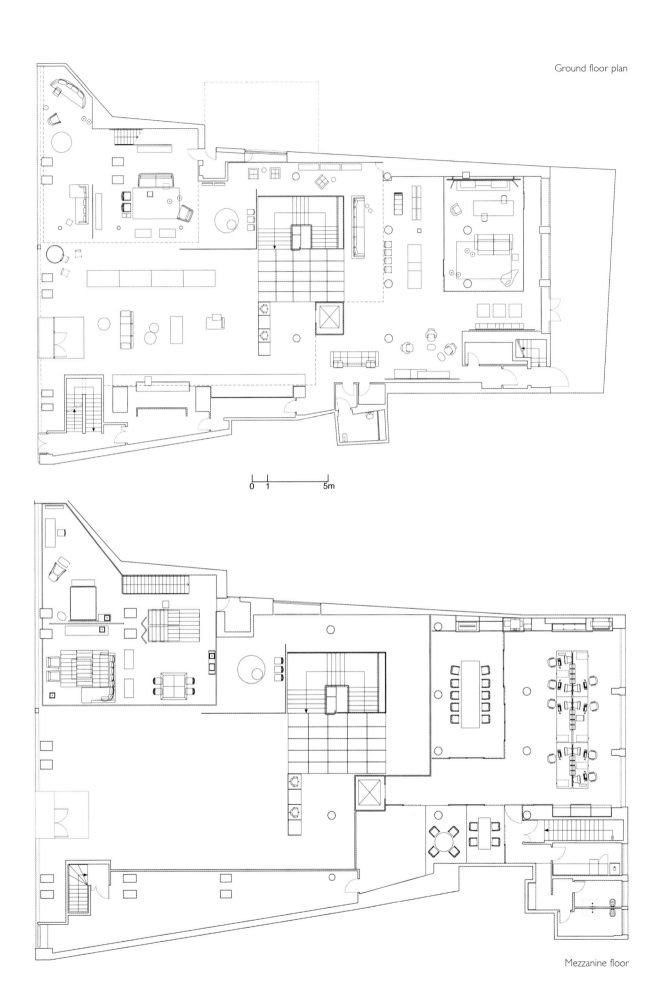

Ground floor plan

0 1   5m

Mezzanine floor

Bohlin Cywinski Jackson & R. Riley
Apple Soho Retail Store

New York City, USA

This new retail store in the heart of New York City's Soho shopping district occupies a 1920's Neo-classical structure that was formerly a U.S. Post Office.

Apple has recently launched a program to build a network of direct retail outlets and the resulting prototype stores, with their maple floors, white fixtures, and an elegant integrated ceiling system, enable consumers to have an up-close, tactile encounter with the products.

A second stage of the client's retail strategy is the development of larger stores in the nation's thriving urban markets, this being the first. The simple palette of the prototype was augmented for SoHo by the addition of stone flooring, bead-blasted stainless steel panels, custom wood fixtures and laminated glass elements. The 16,000 square foot store is centered around a 15-foot-high clear glass staircase, a glass bridge, and a 70-foot-long skylight. Cantilevered glass guardrails allow clear views of second floor spaces. The glass treads of the staircase draw visitors upstairs by playing on one's tactile curiosity to experience the feeling of "walking on air". The top of the treads are diamond-plate fritted for safety and etched for modesty.

At the store's second level, calming dark gray fabric walls and carpet, coupled with luxurious fixed seating, enhance the experience of the demonstration theater. Flanking the stair well are hardware and software displays, and a "Genius" bar.

The bar, display platforms, and seating throughout the store are solid, simply detailed maple tables and benches that balance the cool, technical character of the space with familiar warmth. Functional aspects of the store such as heating/cooling, lighting, security and acoustics are integrated into the design of the ceiling system.

Photographs: Peter Aaron/ESTO

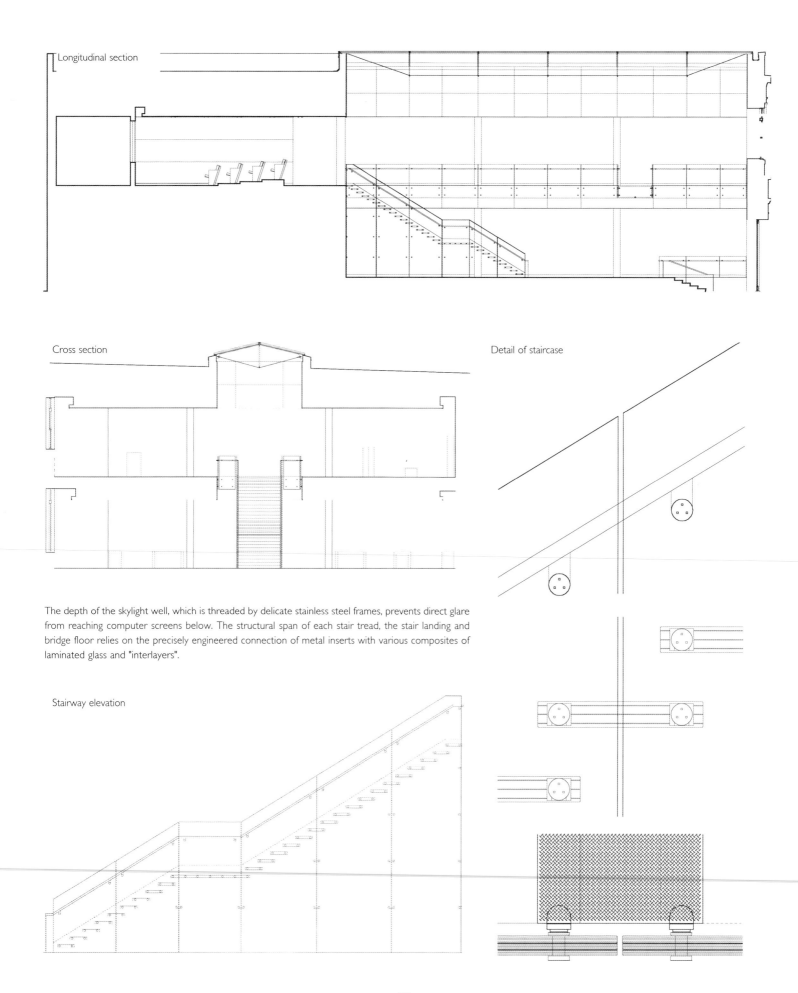

Longitudinal section

Cross section

Detail of staircase

The depth of the skylight well, which is threaded by delicate stainless steel frames, prevents direct glare from reaching computer screens below. The structural span of each stair tread, the stair landing and bridge floor relies on the precisely engineered connection of metal inserts with various composites of laminated glass and "interlayers".

Stairway elevation

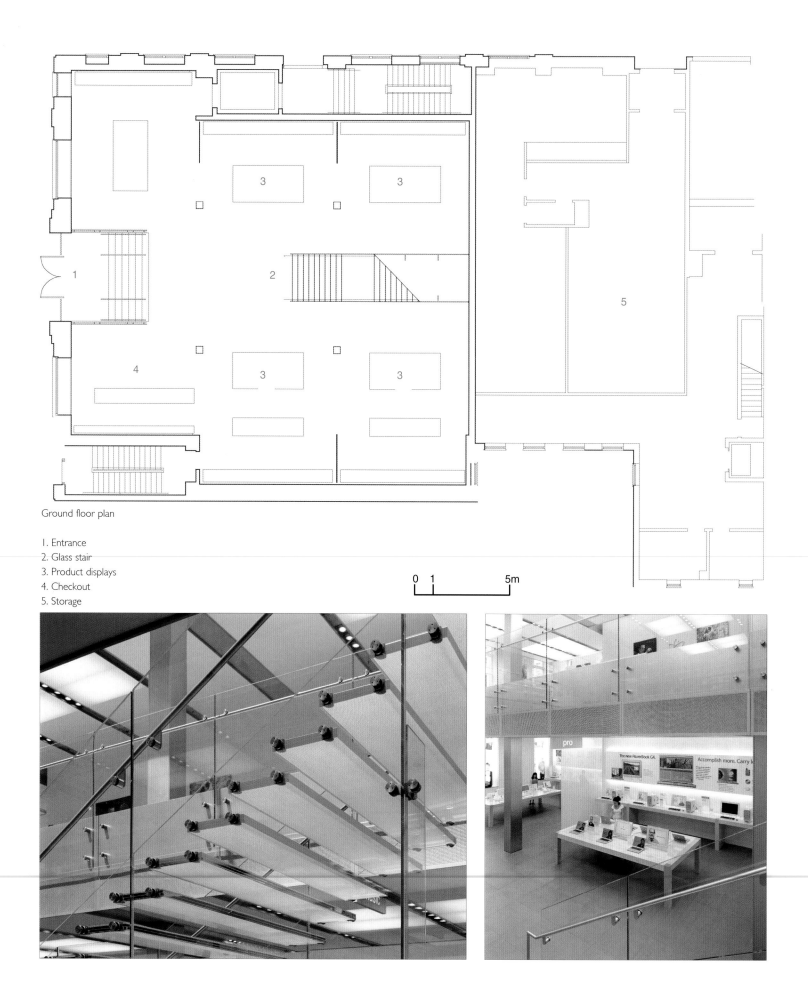

Ground floor plan

1. Entrance
2. Glass stair
3. Product displays
4. Checkout
5. Storage

0 1   5m

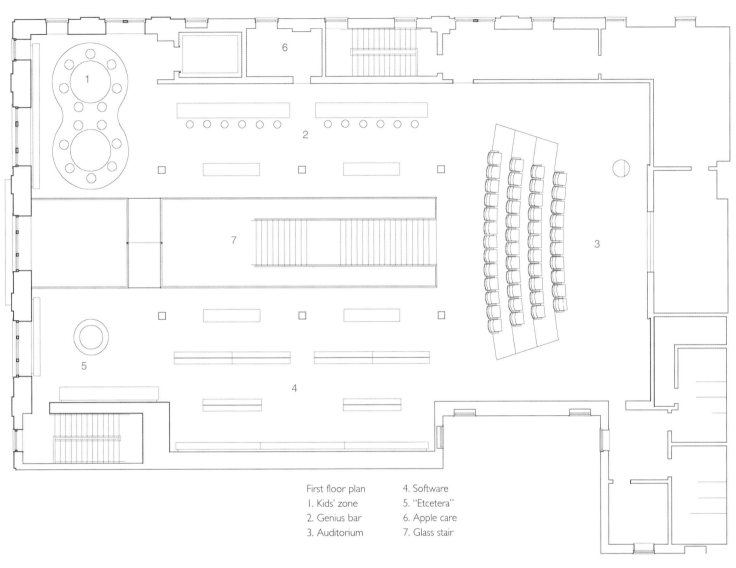

First floor plan
1. Kids' zone
2. Genius bar
3. Auditorium
4. Software
5. "Etcetera"
6. Apple care
7. Glass stair

Lazzarini Pickering Architetti
Fendi

Paris, France

This Rome-based architectural practice was engaged by Fendi to develop the new international image of its boutiques worldwide. The display elements in this shop create architecture rather than merely fill a space. These elements (shelves, tables and horizontal and vertical hanging fascias) have been proportionately scaled according to the dimensions of the space. The shelves measure up to 10 meters long, the tables up to 7, and the hanging fascias may be up to 20 meters in length.

The entire boutique revolves around the staircase, which is crossed by metal elements that mark its progress upward in various directions. A series of display units were custom-designed for the project; as a whole, these bear a clearly defined geometry, yet they are differentiated by the use of materials, such as dark wood, wax-finished iron, prism mirror and glass tops.

The space and position of each boutique will require a different architectural configuration of these display elements. This means that the many Fendi Boutiques around the world are instantly recognizable, while being inherently different, making each a unique spatial and shopping experience and also open to incorporating local architectural traditions and materials.

The configuration of the shelves, fascias and tables encourages an informal display arrangement and movement through the store. Coats are hung or laid out in an apparently casual but sculptural way.

The use of traditional and humble, low-tech materials offers the possibility of trying out new finishes. Rough rendered surfaces are finished with a varnish normally used to protect metal surfaces; the crude iron is first treated with a nitrate solvent to make it virtually stainless and is then finished in wax.

Photographs: Mateo Piazza

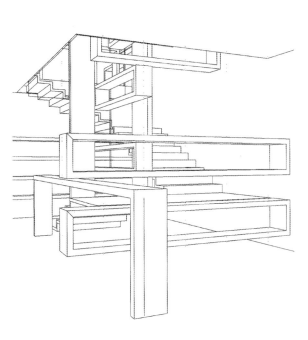

The entire boutique revolves around the staircase, which is crossed by metal elements that mark its progress upward in various directions. A series of display units were custom-designed for the project; as a whole, these bear a clearly defined geometry, yet they are differentiated by the use of materials, such as dark wood, wax-finished iron, prism mirror and glass tops.

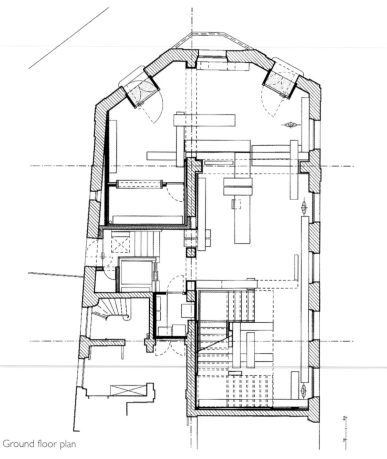

Ground floor plan

44

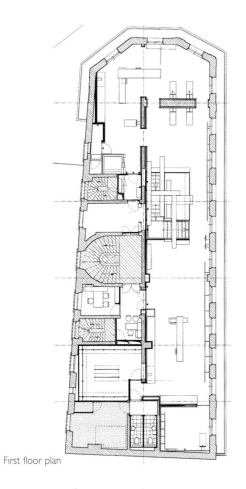

First floor plan

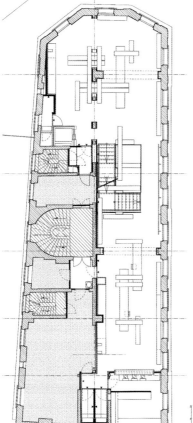

Second floor plan

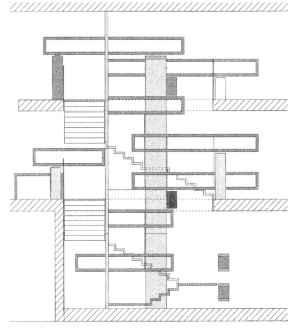

Cross sections

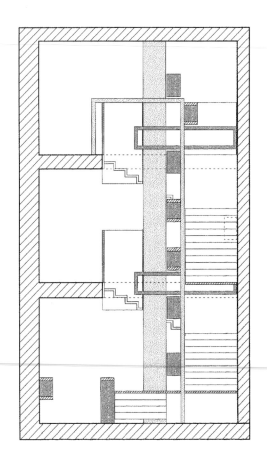

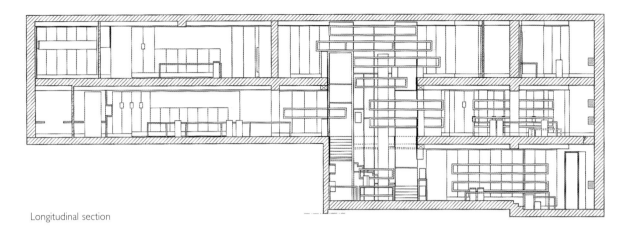

Longitudinal section

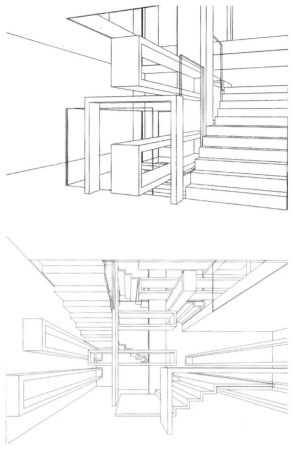

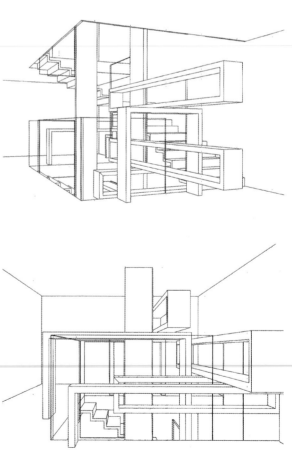

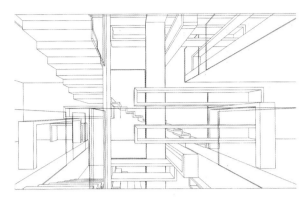

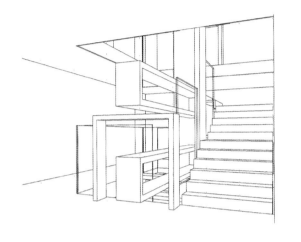

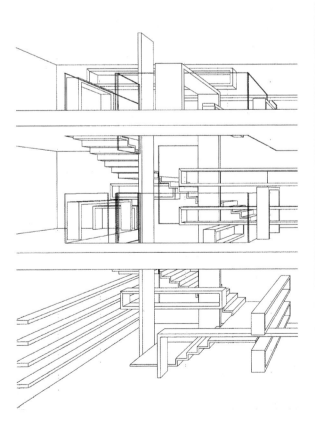

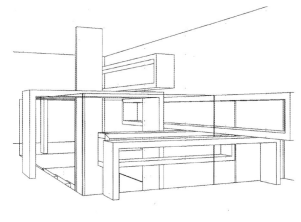

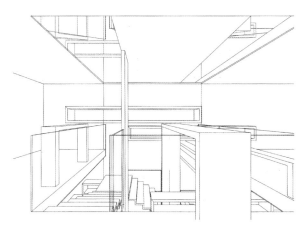

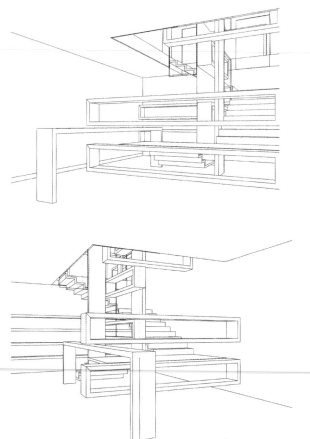

The use of traditional and humble, low-tech materials fits in with the idea of keeping the style informal and also provides the possibility of trying out new finishes. Rough rendered surfaces have been finished with a varnish normally used to protect metal surfaces; the crude iron is first treated with a nitrate solvent to make it virtually stainless and is then finished in wax.

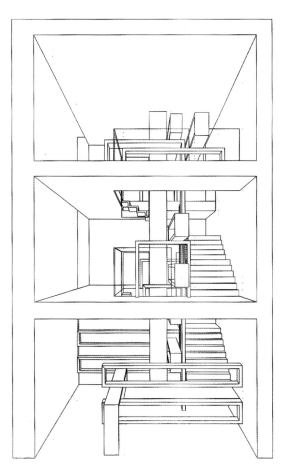

Venturi, Scott Brown & Associates
Exxon Gas Station for Disney World

Florida, USA

Venturi & Scott Brown have designed a prototypical gas station, a perfect and virtuoso interplay in which all the elements that normally define a gas station are combined, and the logo or name of the petrol company is a secondary element in the design of the generic roadside elements.

The solution that was adopted is that of a conventional canopy and large-scale-gas pump structure, which are connected to a self-service shop with large-scale graphics of the word EATS in a translucent frit applied to the inside of the glass curtain wall. Behind the gas station in the garden, characterised by an outer wall whose profile recalls the silhouette of the trees located just behind it.

Two optional solutions were adopted to provide a rapid view of the service area form any point of the road. They are both monumental solutions: 30-foot high, three-dimensional letters spelling "Gas" and a 75-foot high "Gas Pump" sign.

Photographs: Matt Wargo

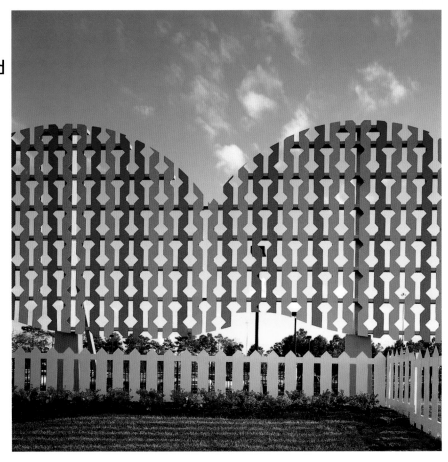

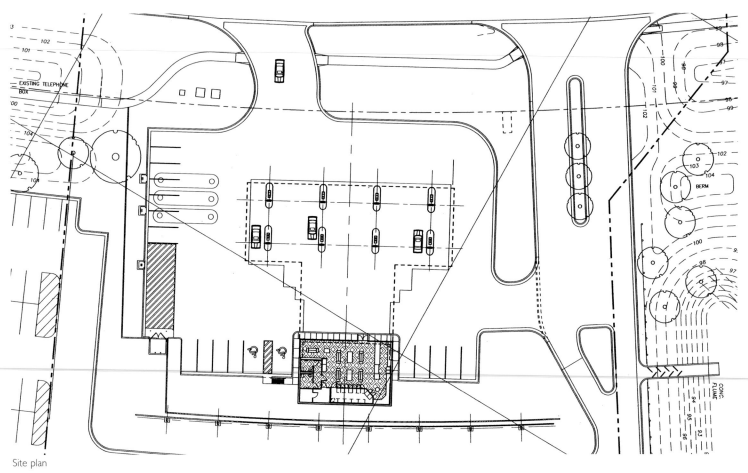

Site plan

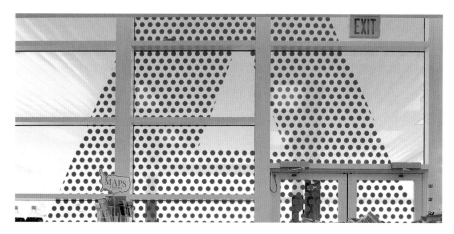

54

Jun Aoki + Eric Carlson
Louis Vuitton

Tokyo, Japan

Tokyo's tree-lined Omotesando Avenue is quickly gaining world renown as a leading street for flagship stores of luxury brands. The commission to design Louis Vuitton's new store, set on a privileged site on the avenue, was won in an international competition; and the doors were opened on the first day of business to over 1400 eager customers.

Inspired by the company's beginnings in the late 1800's as a luggage manufacturer, the designers struck upon the idea of creating a structure composed of an immense stack of randomly piled "trunks".

The delicately shimmering façade was created using a combination of finely woven metal mesh, steel panels polished to a mirror-like sheen and glass etched with a striped pattern. The overall effect deliberately mimics a fine moiré.

Originally used in the manufacture of industrial conveyer belts, this fine metal mesh is also used in the interior. In three varying densities, it has been painted cream and red and is found draped along walls, windows and stairwell voids, recreating in the interior the building's exterior moiré-like aspect. The dual skin system used on the façade is used for the dividing walls inside the store; here, though, lighting has been inserted between the two layers.

The façade's implied stacked trunks also continue in the volumes of the interior, where each space has been treated as its own independent unit, rather than designing each floor in a uniform manner. Custom-designed retail fixtures designed by Louis Vuitton's architecture department fill the spaces, just as they do in the company's Paris headquarters, thus granting a trademark look to an otherwise entirely original design scheme. A dramatic multipurpose hall on the top floor displays a markedly different design scheme. With luxurious white velvet ceilings and cream-colored terrazzo flooring, the only identifiable element linking it to the rest of the store is the subtle inclusion along the windows of the same fine metal weave found throughout the building.

Photographs: Ano Daici, N. Naka

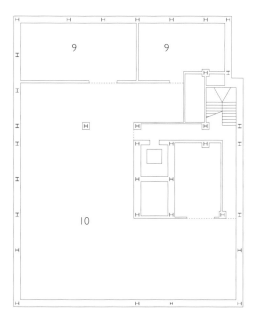

Second basement floor

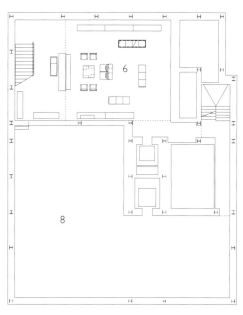

First basement floor

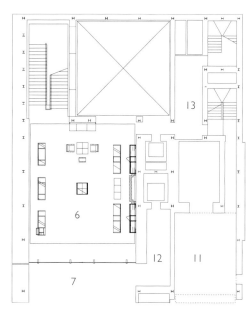

Ground floor plan

1. Louis Vuitton Hall
2. Celux (Member's salon)
3. Office
4. Louis Vuitton Salon
5. Terrace
6. Retail (Shop)
7. Entrance
8. Beauty salon
9. Machine room
10. Parking
11. Car Entrance
12. Sub entrance hall
13. Storage
14. Repair room
15. Pantry

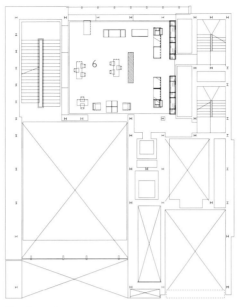

First floor plan

Second floor plan

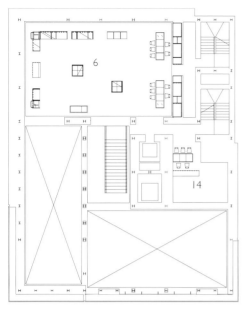

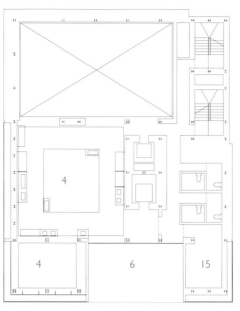

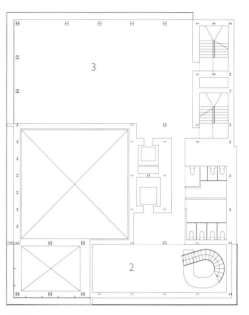

Third floor plan

Fourth floor plan

Fifth floor plan

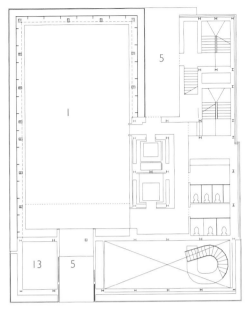

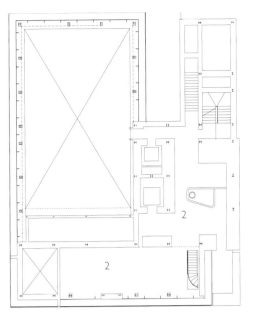

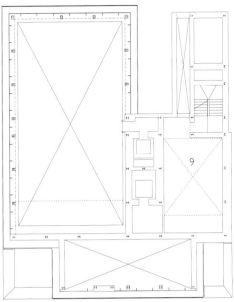

Sixth floor plan

Seventh floor plan

Eighth floor plan

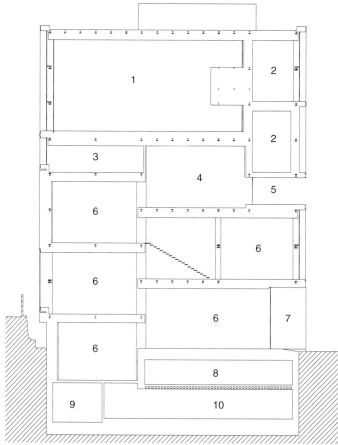

1. Louis Vuitton Hall
2. Celux (Member's salon)
3. Office
4. Louis Vuitton Salon
5. Terrace
6. Retail (Shop)
7. Entrance
8. Beauty salon
9. Machine room
10. Parking

Ground floor plan

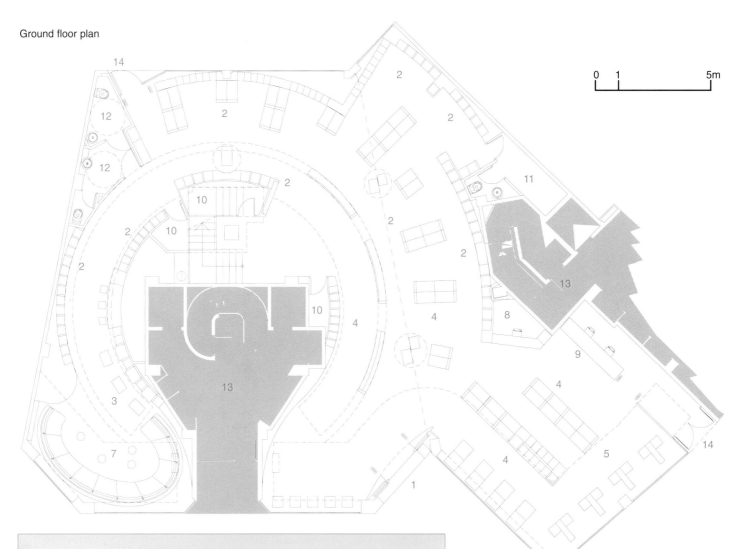

0 1   5m

1. Entrance
2. Books
3. Book consultation
4. Music
5. Listening area
6. Cafeteria
7. Lounge

8. Customer service
9. Checkout counter
10. Storage
11. Changing rooms
12. Toilets
13. Vestibule neighboring building
14. Exit

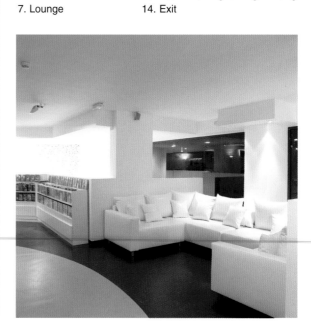

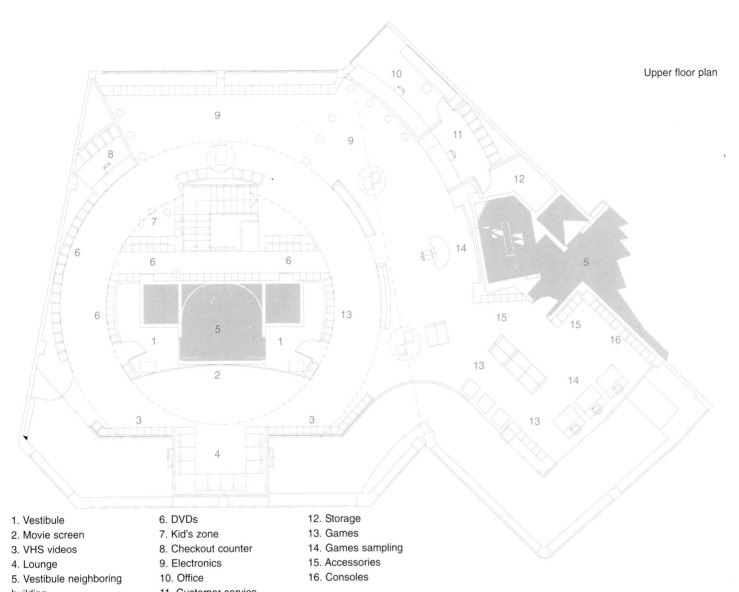

1. Vestibule
2. Movie screen
3. VHS videos
4. Lounge
5. Vestibule neighboring building
6. DVDs
7. Kid's zone
8. Checkout counter
9. Electronics
10. Office
11. Customer service
12. Storage
13. Games
14. Games sampling
15. Accessories
16. Consoles

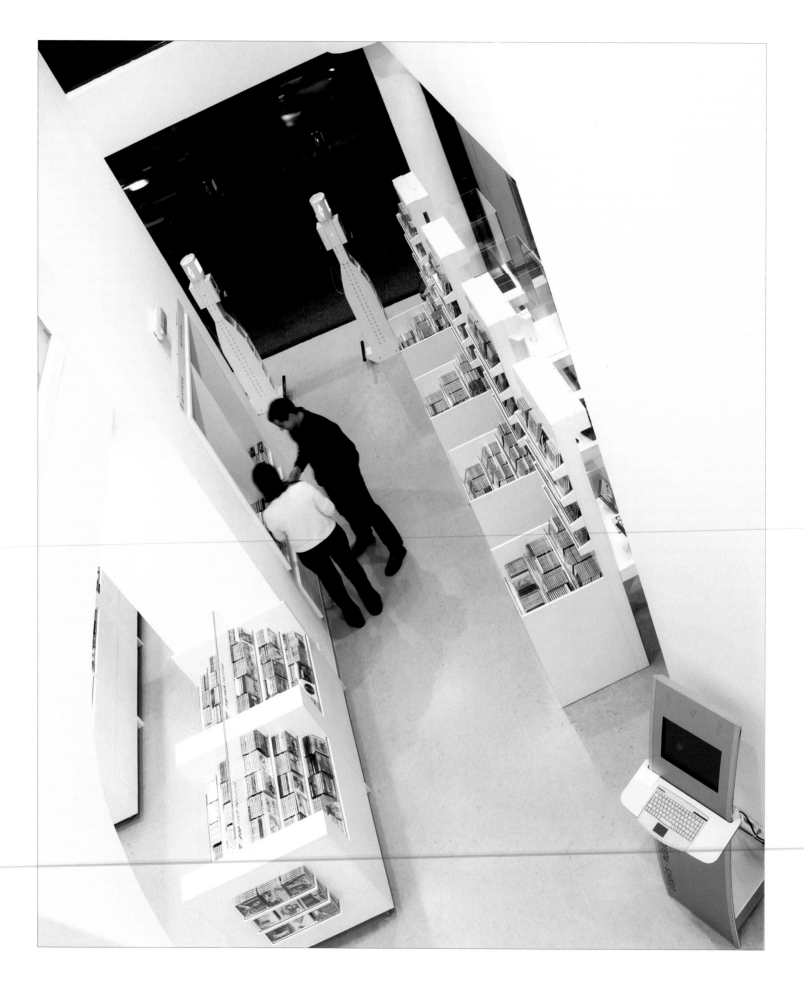

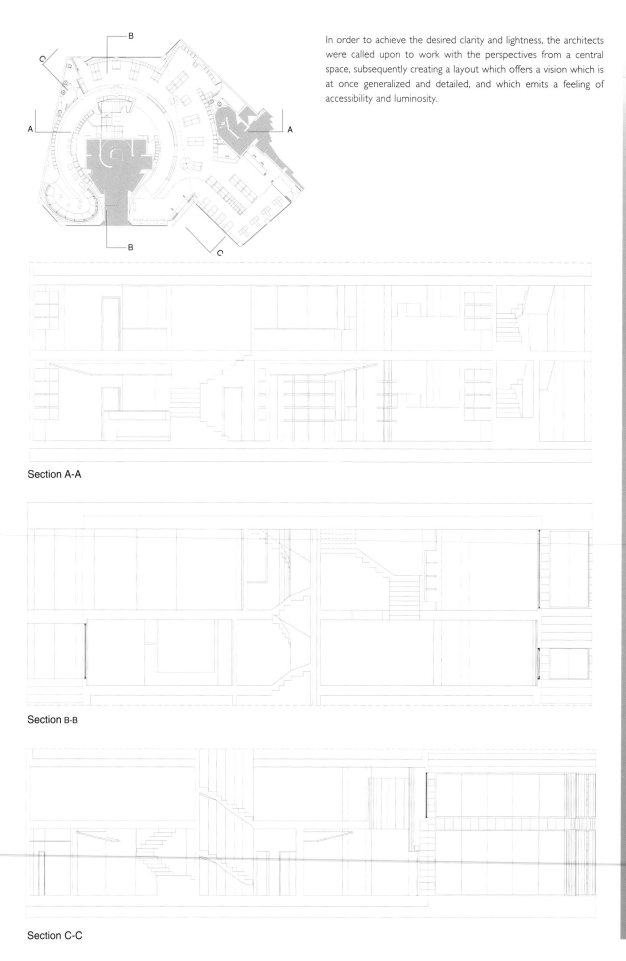

In order to achieve the desired clarity and lightness, the architects were called upon to work with the perspectives from a central space, subsequently creating a layout which offers a vision which is at once generalized and detailed, and which emits a feeling of accessibility and luminosity.

Section A-A

Section B-B

Section C-C

John Pawson
Calvin Klein

Paris, France

This is the latest in a series of collaborations between Calvin Klein and John Pawson, the first being the renowned clothing designer's first shop in New York, followed by projects in Tokyo, Seoul and London. The design of each shop is based primarily on the existing architecture of the interior, although trademark elements are included to tie them together.

As in the trend-setting New York store, the Paris shop features austere white walls and York stone floor cladding. Pawson has custom designed a line of furniture built from Douglas fir and ebonized mahogany, materials he has used in other Klein stores for fixtures as well.

The Paris store has to accommodate a complex range of merchandise: clothes for both women and men, cosmetics, shoes, and a collection for the home. They need to be given their own defined areas and be shown in different ways without losing long, uninterrupted internal spatial vistas.

With rather less space than was available to him in New York and a circulation plan defined by a central T-shaped staircase, Pawson has concentrated the women's collection on the ground floor, with menswear and the home collection in their own areas on the upper story.

The levels are linked by the main stair, set in a double-height space defined by a full-height light slot cut into the stair wall, hinting at what is above and suggesting the possibility of alternative destinations.

Pawson works with space and light to create a place that simultaneously beguiles and serves its customers. The process of finding a garment, trying it on and paying for is made as straightforward as possible, while the spatial qualities of the environment in which this takes place are heightened. And that, in essence, is what gives every Pawson store for Klein its common identity.

Photographs: Vincent Knapp

Ground floor plan

First floor plan

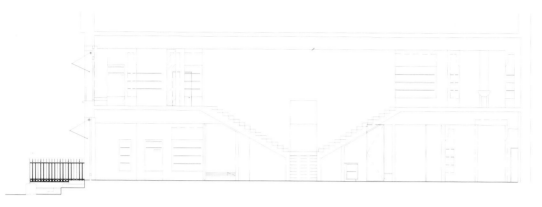

Section AA

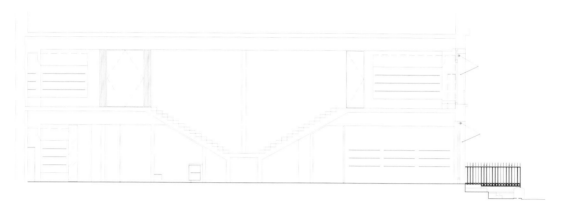

Section BB

The materials used are classic and simple, with sandblasted glass shelves and York stone flooring in a neutral tone combined with custom-designed furniture in mahogany and Douglas fir. The austere white walls terminate at their base in a three-millimeter gap where they meet the stone floor.

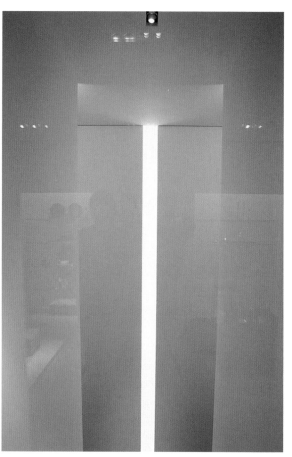

Longitudinal section

0   1   2m

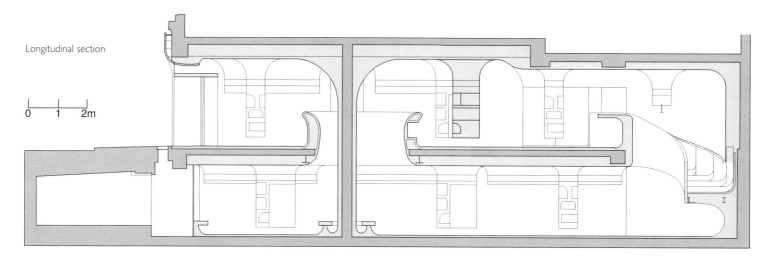

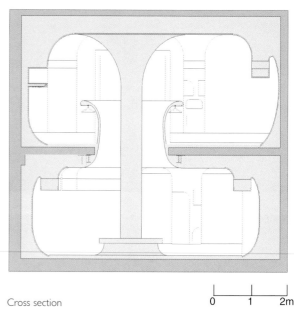

Cross section

0   1   2m

Suspended above a circular platform set aside for displaying footwear is an engraved Victorian-style glass box housing McQueen's debut fragrance, Kingdom. An elegant terrazzo staircase, which has been patterned after the interior of a fossilized shell, leads to the lower floor.

3deluxe
D'Fly Jewelry Store

New York City, USA

The New York jewelry store D'fly owes its heterogeneous spatial impact to the contrast between emphatically tech-functional features and the organic forms of "genetic architecture".

Even a first glance through the shop window enthralls the passer-by: a fascinating and uniquely intense, nearly lab-like atmosphere cast almost entirely in white. The interior of the shop has the feel of an artificial implant on 47 Greene Street - the original shell is a listed building in the style typical of Soho.

The optical effects are further enhanced by the pneumatic noises made by sixteen remote controlled showcases which, when their opening mechanism is triggered, evoke an almost industrial high-tech atmosphere. Artificial muscles help raise their heavy glass lids 40 cm, enabling the selected piece of jewelry to be removed.

The shop is clearly divided length-wise into three consecutive zones. In the front third, as part of the genetic architecture evident throughout the shop, there is a small lounge, adding a touch of coziness and private charm to the otherwise rational atmosphere. The soft lighting, with its gradually changing color tones, emphasizes that this is an area where you can relax and enjoy taking your time.

The diagonal front of the desk directly opposite skillfully steers customers toward the middle section of the room, where attention is focused solely on displaying the goods. Here, the lighting turns sober, guiding the eye more to the products. Architecturally, the area is accentuated by projections on the walls and ceiling that seem to grip the room in the middle like a clasp. The showcases, arranged lengthwise at eye height, emphasize the unifying character of this section of the room.

Once through, you reach the try-on area, characterized once again by "genetic architecture" and colorful, moving light. A bamboo garden integrated into the rear wall lends the place a special charm. The try-on counter provides further technical finesse: by means of a remote-controlled extending mechansim, three mirrors slide silently out of the counter's corpus. They form a surprisingly private setting for both customer and personal sales advisor for the duration of the fitting. The innumerable reflections of the bamboo plants can be seen in the mirrors and the glass of the neighboring showcases, bringing the shop owner's home country of Taiwan to mind.

Photographs: James Wilkins

Each of the sixteen custom-designed display cases is lit from within by a combination of halogen and fluorescent lamps set into the light boxes, which are composed of stainless steel elements and tempered glass. A peripheral slit has been left open to let heat from the lamps escape. The glass doors of the display cases are remote control operated, thereby eliminating the need for keys.

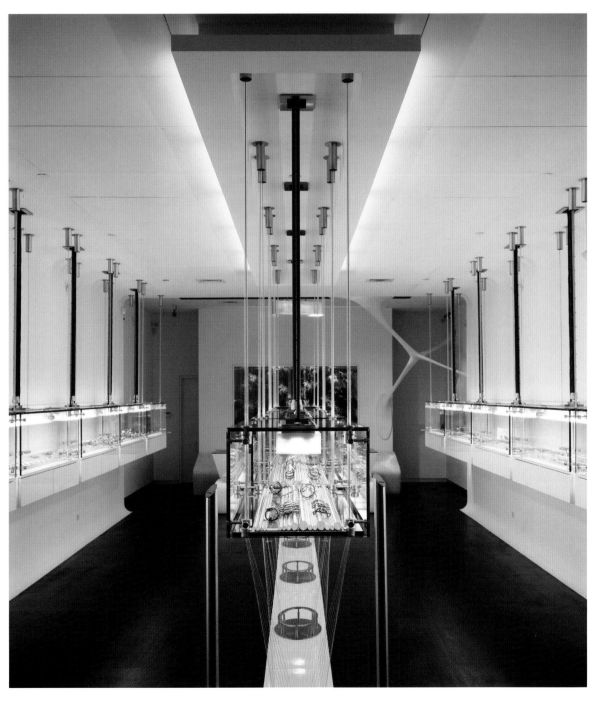

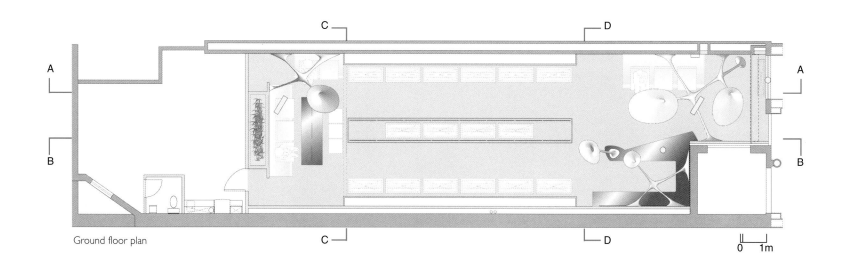

Ground floor plan

0   1m

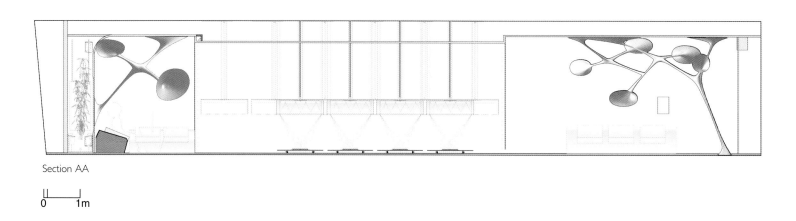

Section AA

0   1m

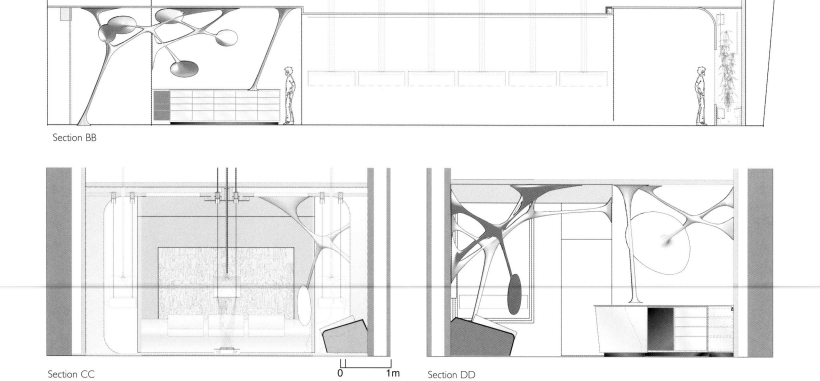

Section BB

Section CC

0   1m

Section DD

Gorgona Boehm Associates
Supermarket Merkur

Wiener Neustadt, Austria

The Viennese architects Gorgona Boehm Associates were faced with a difficult project: converting a food market with all the charm of an industrial shed, providing space for individual traders and a restaurant, replacing the facades and adding a parking bay. The middle section of the roof was partly removed and a new exterior steel construction with suspended glass panels illuminates a piazetta whose center is formed by a restaurant, around which the food market and the individual businesses forma U-shape.

Here the customers can meet, relax and enjoy the restaurant's fare. But the restaurant and food block also form a central axis that relates to the glazed roof. The existing elements are revalued by the precise new design, especially in the conduction of light by the reflectors. The abstract form of the structure avoids competing with the flood of signs from the commercial world.

The eighty-meter entrance facade becomes an intelligent image of innovative architectural solutions. A two-layer perforated metal structure in front of the black building shell produces a striking interference effect through the use of neon. The small black holes become moving strips that accompany the observers as they go past, or lead them into a perspective of endless profundity as they approach.

At night the fabric of light disguises the substance of the building, dissolving it into a variety of levels of perception. But as one goes into the large entrance hall, the wide space of the interior stands out in contrast to the high-tech facade illumination. The solution of the parking bay on one side of the building is also clear and empirical. The light slits are arranged vertically, establishing a dynamic movement and enhancing the black box of the store with their unusual natural light. The architectural message is also conveyed by the coloring. The aluminum grey links the load-bearing parts inwards and outwards to form a whole.

Photographs: Margheritta Spiluttini

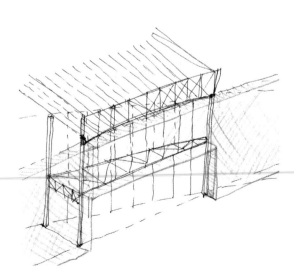

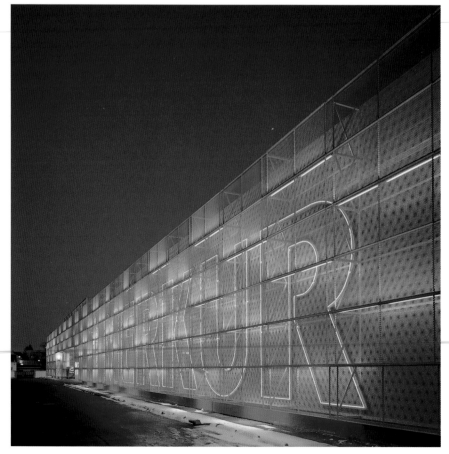

97

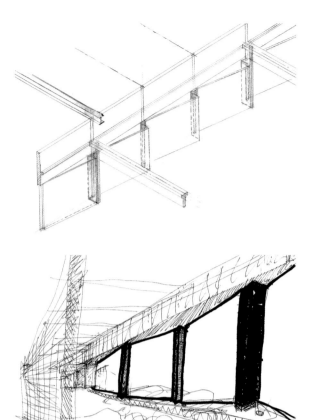

Rei Kawakubo
Comme des Garçons

New York, USA / Tokyo, Japan

The two new Comme des Garçons boutiques in New York and Tokyo propose a new concept for commercial spaces: instead of a rarefied atmosphere and minimalist facilities, these spaces seek to create complicity between the designer and the customers, interaction between the person and the space.

The headquarters of Comme des Garçons in New York has moved to the district of Chelsea. This new location inspires the special characteristics of the boutique: it is a building without windows, with an external lining of brick and a fire exit. Except for the mouth of the tunnel with its strange red lights and the white wall at the bottom, nothing hints at the presence of a space like Comme des Garçons. The tunnel is the element that defines the space and summarizes its conceptual design: the idea is to create a feeling of expectation that leads to the active participation of the customers. This aluminum tunnel with a monocoque structure does not require ribs or braces. The lamps fitted into the floor guide the visitor towards the interior of the space. A swinging glass door marks the entrance to the enclosure, and a blind protects the entrance at night.

For the Aoyama shop, in Tokyo, the façade was renovated with walls of corrugated glass covered by a blue screen that isolates the shop and increases the curiosity of potential customers. The interior door leads to a space impregnated with the architect's personality. The idea that the client should not come into contact with the clothes immediately is central, so the space has been distributed in such a way that the garments are not immediately visible. The field of vision is blocked by large irregular structures of white-painted steel. According to Kawakubo, hiding the clothes means that the customers have to look for them themselves, in their own time. An atmosphere of tension is thus created. The corridors run through a succession of curved walls that lead to different spaces. Each of the spaces, decorated by the artists Christian Astugueivieille and Sophie Smallhorn, is conceived as a work of art that corresponds to a different atmosphere and product.

Photographs: Masayuki Hayashi & Todd Eberle

Ground floor plan

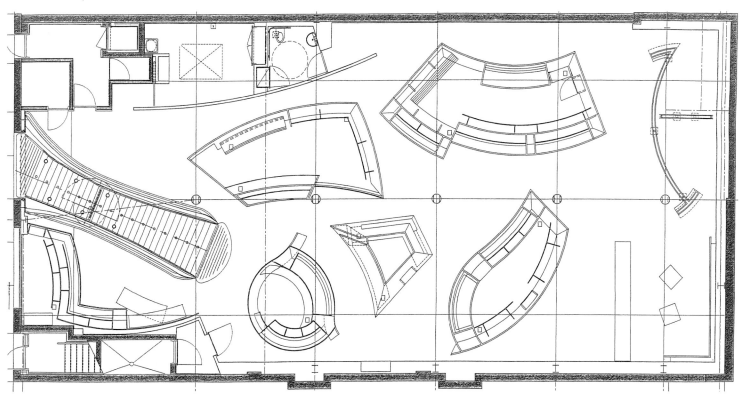

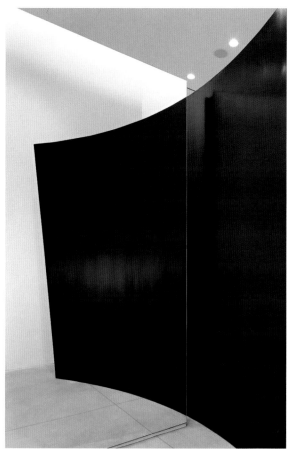
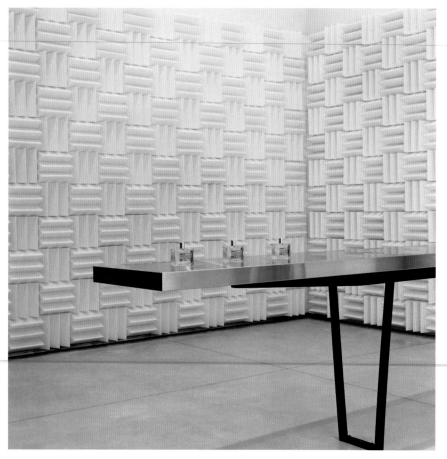

Tokyo

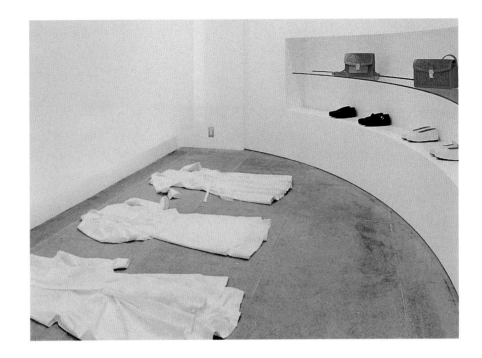

Floor plan

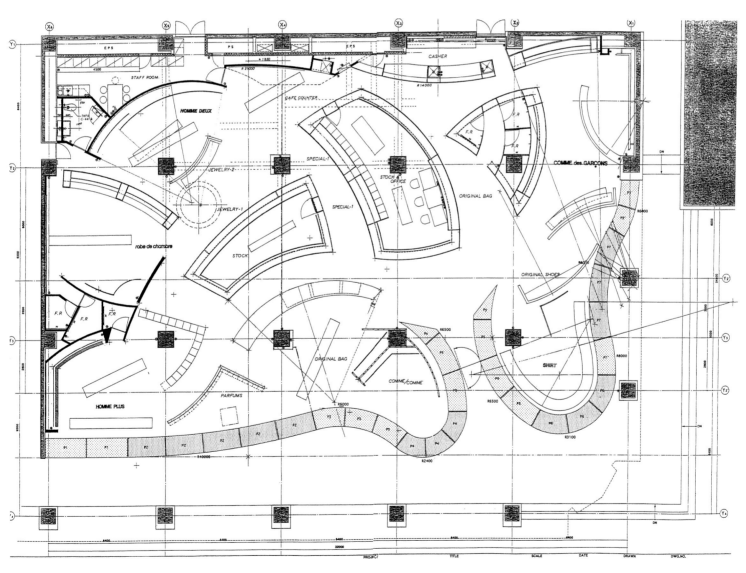

The varied treatment of the walls distinguishes the different exhibition spaces. Christian Astuguevieille and Sophie Smallhorn designed two of these spaces and Kawakubo designed the rest.

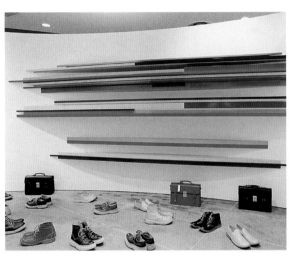

The new façade of corrugated glass covered by a dotted blue screen was designed by Future Systems of London. Passers-by can see some of the clothes through the screen, but privacy is a major feature of the interior.

NL Architects for Droog Design
Mandarina Duck Flagship Store

Paris, France

Mandarina Duck will extend its impressive reputation in the field of designer bags with a collection of clothes and accessories, the so-called small items. The reinvention of its identity (a perpetual process in the fashion industry) requires a new shop design to present the new product lines. Since shopping became the number one distraction of the contemporary urbanite, all important labels and brands are in a battle to create the most convincing environment for this new form of entertainment. The new ideas are launched and tested in flagship stores or ambassador shops. From these focal points of exchange the new identity spreads bit by bit over the local stores.

This notion was the starting point for "a store with no architecture"; that is, a shop that consists of furniture and products only. These will be orchestrated in any chosen environment, in any hull. The relatively "light" elements will determine the display and atmosphere. If they turn out to be successful they can be used in other MD shops as well. By using a catalogue of specifically designed Mandarina Duck furniture and inserting it into a specific spatial condition every new shop can be identified as MD but still appear very different from all the others.

Space can be considered the biggest luxury of all. In many stores this is apparent in the virtual absence of sellable items. The objective is to stress the exclusivity of the brand. The aim of the new shop is to create a series of freestanding objects that are "countable": the Cocoons. They impart a sense of spaciousness but at the same time hold numerous products in their interiors. The pod-like, futuristic inverted clothing racks, for example, are smooth and bare on the outside, with the merchandise contained within a walk-in space. The shop looks empty, but is full.

Photographs: Ralph Kämena

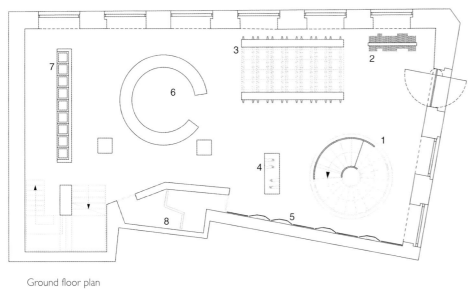

Ground floor plan

0 1 2m

First floor plan

1. Revolving Stair
2. Pinwall
3. Pallet Tunnel
4. Incubator
5. Rubber Wall
6. Inverse Clothrack
7. Counter
8. Fitting Rooms
9. Vacuumwall
10. Epoxy-cupboard
11. Stacked round tables
12. Curtain Room
13. Socle
14. Fluo-cupboards
15. Mirrorboxes
16. Grassland

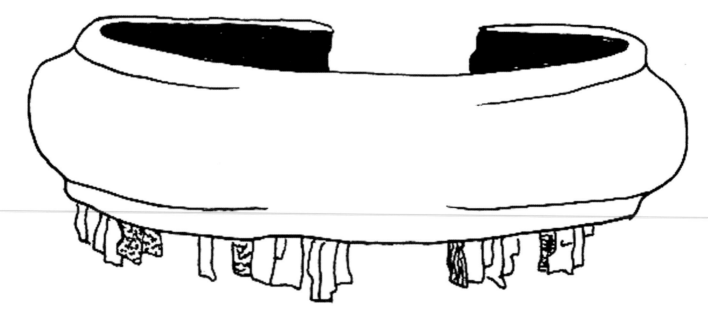

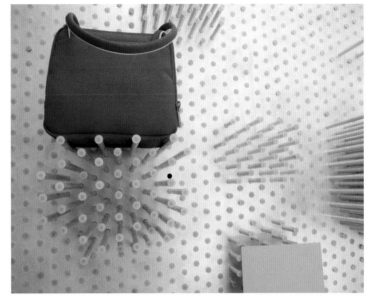

Javier Maroto & Álvaro Soto
La Oreja de Plata II

Madrid, Spain

The jeweler's store La Oreja de Plata II, for the designer Chus Burés, occupies two floors, with the Calle Jorge Juan entry level measuring just 7 m² in area, and a lower space of approximately 40 m². The architects decided to make the entrance floor a void from which one descends a transparent staircase, so that the space would be revealed slowly. In fact, the architects imagined that the whole entrance would be experienced as if inside a shop window that customers would not leave until they had gone down to the lower floor. In this movement, visitors are accompanied by display cabinets and glass boxes suspended from the ceiling onto which light is projected. The jewels and the objects are thus exposed to view, casting evocative shades on the glass supports.

On the lower floor there is a rectangular room ("a Mediterranean space", as Chus Burés called it) that is gently lit from above, reminiscent of the way light falls on the clear walls of a southern courtyard. The floor is of dark wooden planks without a skirting board, and creaks under the feet of the customers.

The architects have created a radical and totally interior space because most of the work was done in the basement. They were interested in the idea of projecting the variable brightness of the natural and artificial light that passes through each cabinet. They converted the small street level entrance space into a skylight that illuminates the lower level of the shop and contains an almost transparent staircase.

Photographs: Juan Merinero

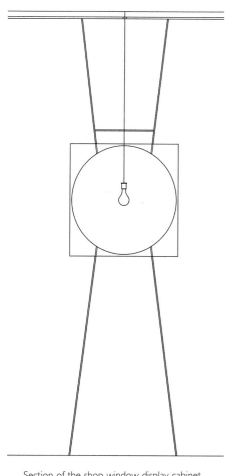

Section of the shop window display cabinet

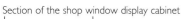
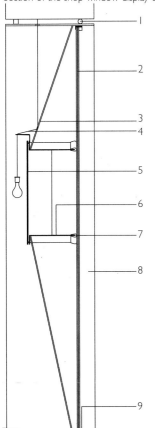

1
2
3
4
5
6
7
8
9
10

1. Neoprene profile
2. 6x5x6 mm STADIP
3. e=6 mm bars
   (welded to the shop
   window frame)
4. e=3 mm bar
5. 3x3 mm STADIP
   white butyral
6. e=3 mm plate
7. Neoprene profile
   supported by glass
8. e=10 mm frame
   polished and varnished
   steel
9. 20x20 mm bowtell
10. 40x20 mm L profile

Access to the shop is through a tiny floor that acts as a shop window. The boundaries between the shop window and the staircases leading to the basement are blurred, creating a bright space in which the elements on display float freely.

Elevation of a back-lit suspended cabinet

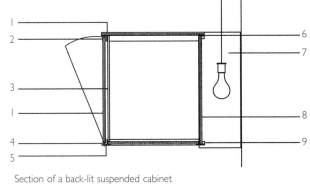

Section of a back-lit suspended cabinet

1. 4x4 mm STADIP transparent butyral
2. 15x10 mm U profile
3. 6 mm diameter bar
4. Bolts
5. e=2 mm T profile
6. 20x20 mm L profile
7. e=3mm painted plate RAL 9006
8. 4x4 mm STADIP white butyral
9. 10x10 mm bowtell

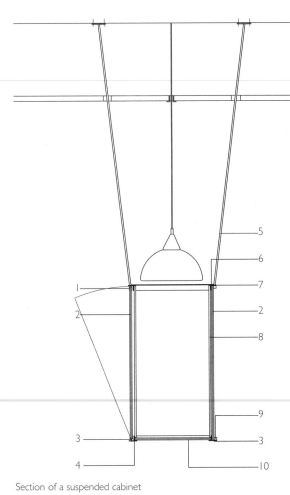

Section of a suspended cabinet

1. 15x10 mm U profile
2. 4x4 mm STADIP transparent butyral
3. Bolts
4. e=3 mm T profile
5. e=6mm bars
6. e=1mm perforated plate
7. 20x20 mm L profile
8. 6 mm bolts
9. 10x10 mm bowtell
10. 4x4 mm STADIP White butyral

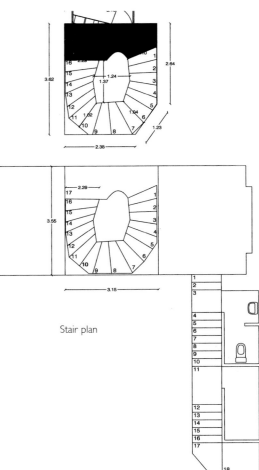

Stair plan

Artificial lighting is projected through the cabinets, transforming them into lamps. They are variable in shape, location and brightness.

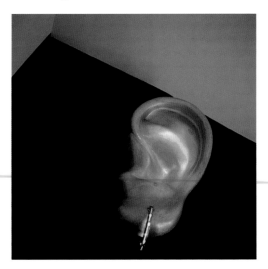

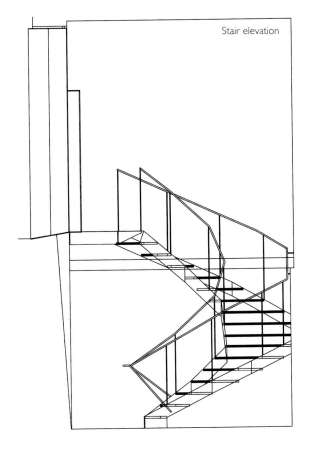

Stair elevation

Michael Gabellini
Jil Sander Boutique

Milan, Italy

This project is not the first time that Michael Gabellini has worked for Jil Sander. His team had previously been hired to design another boutique in San Francisco and some offices and a show-room in Hamburg for this same company. This project called for a single-story design for a shop in which to display the women's and men's clothing and accessory collections. The design concept emphasized simplicity and comfort for customers, who can view and try on the collections on display. The boutique's only street entrance is located on the façade between four wide display windows that entice passers by to enter the space and view its wares, while at the same time providing the space with an abundance of natural light. This light reinforces the compression of certain areas and suggests a continuity between the boutique's interior and its surroundings.

All interior vertical surfaces have been polished and painted white, conferring a bright, luminous effect on the space. Built-in lamps placed directly above each display highlight the quality of the clothes and guide the customer through the boutique. A steel staircase connects the showroom floor to a small storage room in the basement where the merchandise not on display is kept.

The display fixtures are an integral part of the interior architecture of this project. The simple and elegant pieces -some steel, others in wood- are distributed throughout the space in such a way as to remain unnoticed, thereby granting the clothing and accessories all due importance. Thus, the merchandise is never eclipsed by its surrounding context. Rather, its quality is enhanced and the customer feels comfortable and is able to enjoy the shopping experience.

Photographs: Alberto Piovano

For this project, the architect designed a space with pure, bare surfaces where the display units, in metal and wood, are sculptural bodies, elements where the clothes are exhibited.

6a architects
Oki-ni

London, UK

Oki-ni has offered the fashion market a fresh relationship between consumer and product. Limited edition clothes by global and independent brands are available only online from Oki-ni. 6a architects won the commission to design the flagship store on Savile Row and the concessions that follow with an installation-based concept that emphasizes the tactile and social opportunities of clothes shopping. Low piles of felt replace the traditional arrangement of shelving, rails and furniture and define Oki-ni's physical landscape; the generous felt surfaces are both display and furniture. This departure from the established conventions of retail design creates a place where resting and socializing play a critical part in the discovery of new products.

With all transactions conducted on-line, the point of sale is also missing. 6A have avoided an explicit concentration of technology and proposed the laptop as a sales interface, gently assimilated amongst products and visitors.

The first and largest Oki-ni store completed by this studio sits on a commanding site at the Conduit Street end of Savile Row. Three large windows reveal a felt landscape contained by a gently sloping oak tray inserted into the existing concrete shell. The fan shaped tray is independent of its site, leaving a series of mysterious spaces that conceal changing room and stairs between the low oak walls and the shell. Clothes hang ambiguously from the low sides of the oak tray with domestic familiarity.

Since opening, this shop has been a success with the public and critics alike and has been recognized as one of the most significant developments in retail design over the last few years.

Photographs: David Grandorge

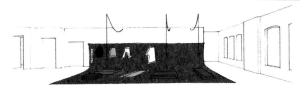

Layout options

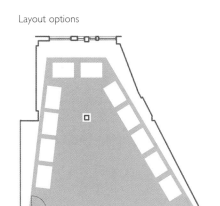

1. Perimeter

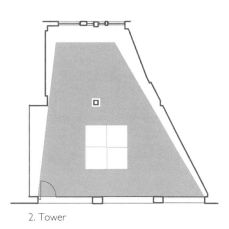

2. Tower

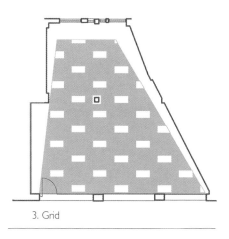

3. Grid

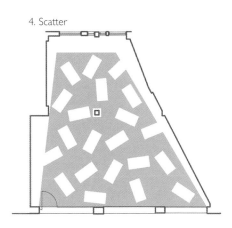

4. Scatter

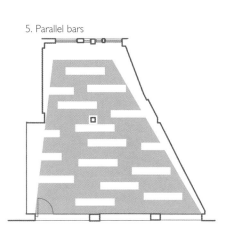

5. Parallel bars

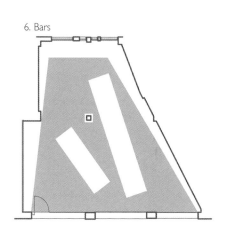

6. Bars

With only the lightest of touches, the raw concrete of the shell is transformed by the oak flooring and wall paneling into an enticing retreat into luxury. The floor slopes upward toward the back of the store, creating a difference in height of just under one meter. The top edge of the wall panels has been set parallel to the slope of the floor to create a seamless visual line from the front of the store to the back.

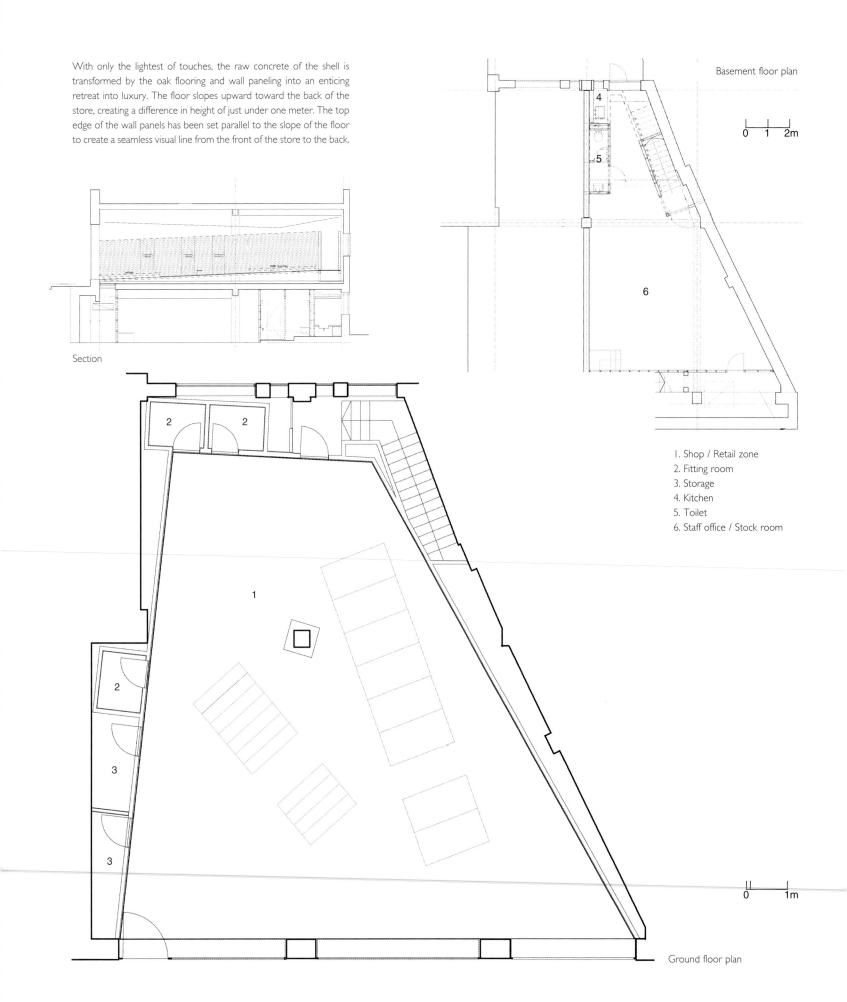

Basement floor plan

0 1 2m

Section

1. Shop / Retail zone
2. Fitting room
3. Storage
4. Kitchen
5. Toilet
6. Staff office / Stock room

0 1m

Ground floor plan

Three large laminated glass windows with stainless steel frames provide ample views from the exterior of the unexpected felt landscape within, contained by a gently sloping oak "tray" inserted in the existing concrete shell.

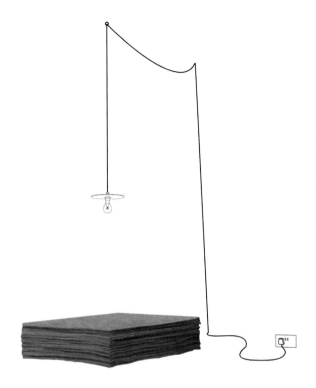

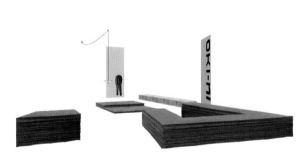

M. Paillard (Unitzone) &
Michel Ferranet
Thierry Mugler

Paris, France

Clean geometry, contrasts in scale and cohesion of forms and materials were the design themes in this program. The studio paid particular attention to the rigor of forms and volumes and to the choice of both materials and lighting in order to grant an overall feeling of fluidity.

Treated in fiber concrete, a highly resistant material usually used in the construction of bridges, the floor stones continue onto the main display wall. The result is a grayish surface, homogeneous in texture and color, its forceful presence determining the space.

A long concrete wall holds nearly three-quarters of the clothes without weighing down the general line of the store. Each space is an open and fluid cell designed in terms of form rather than merely function. Working with the functionality of each support, new uses were sought.

Echoing the rich, noble and dense fabrics of the collection, concrete, buffed stainless steel in a mat and satin finish as well as a rare wood, swamp oak, were the primary decorative materials chosen. Bringing together refined and raw materials gives contemporary, sophisticated effects in a harmony of grays and browns.

A new furniture concept called the "jeté" disrupts the perspective of the store. Given men's tendency to scatter their clothes rather than put them away, an alternative to the traditional rack is offered here: sheathed, seamless foam structures in dark, smoky tones. These elements can be leaned against or used to drape clothes over. They can be set up and folded away simply and elegantly.

Neutral shades that would enable an ample margen for working with the lighting were used. As with the furniture, the lighting is completely integrated into the architecture.

Conceived in the spirit of a lounge, the basement space is equipped with comfortable furniture: leather armchairs by Jasper Morrison, rugs and TV screens, all providing a relaxing setting where visitors can wait while clothes are tried on or altered.

Photographs: Marc Domage

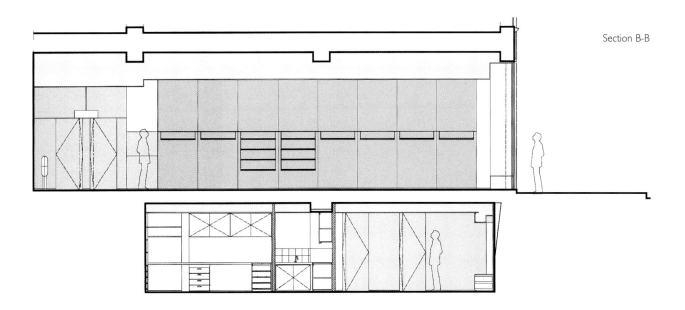

Section B-B

```
0    1    2              5 m
```

Section C-C

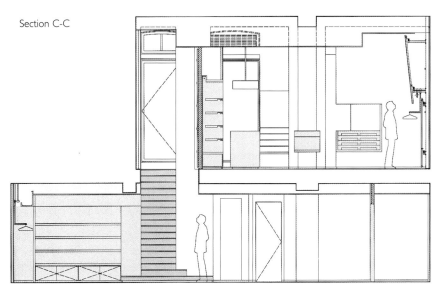

The volume is punctuated by such custom-designed objects as the standard lamp or "jeté", the latter being free-standing sculptural elements which are used as alternatives to clothing racks where customers can leave clothes lying once they have been tried on. Materials such as swamp oak and buffed stainless steel in a mat and satin finish echo the rich fabrics of the shop's collection.

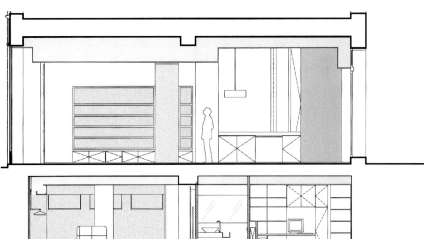

Section D-D

Detail of street-side façade

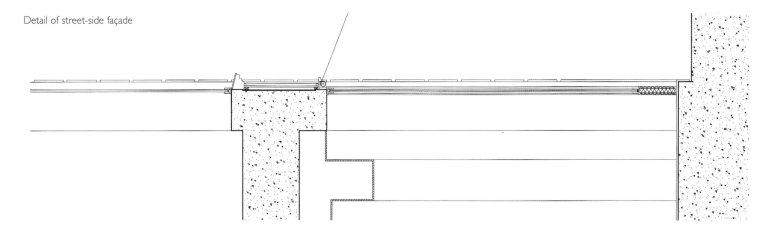

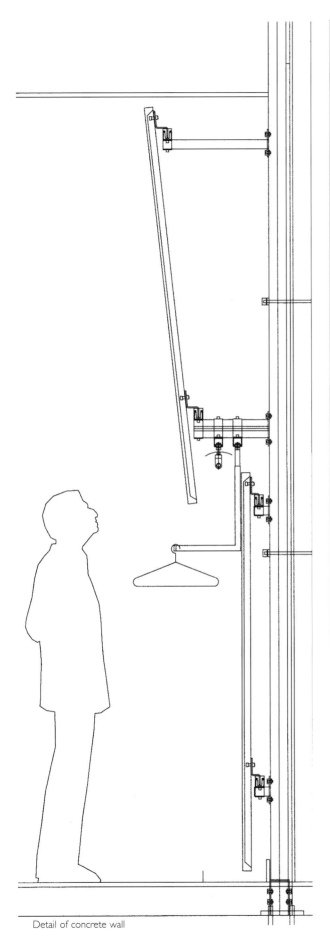

Detail of concrete wall

Dosseret droit

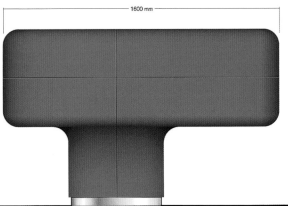

Dosseret angulaire

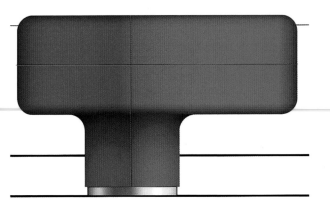

Agustí Costa
Bakery Passeig 40

Berga, Spain

The clients stipulated a very basic program: a shop with display cases, refrigerated cabinets and six-person tasting tables, as well as a wok area for creating the products and a small service area. In this project, the designer worked with an interplay of textures and plastic effects in an attempt to combine the geometric wealth with a diversity of forms, colors and nuances.

The creation of this unique space was governed by the idea of the void. A unitary box enclosed by walls with diverse finishes, reduced but filled with uses, where lighting, display units and a tasting area are all integrated, forming a deep display window that ends with the work area. This box features niches, cabinets, drawers, a long built-in countertop and a curtain, as well as fixtures which are instrumental in the storage, display and sampling of the products.

Two parallel lines organize the length-wise sides, with walls that start at the street and stretch into the depth of the shop to end at the work area, adapting and acquiring, along their length, the adequate treatment. Thus, to the left, past the display window, the walls are of a smooth finish and provide the support for four cantilevered platforms. This same wall becomes a cabinet and features a change in texture in the display area, taking on sales functions, before entering the work area, which is an open container where the functions are concealed behind screens of the same material, here serving to diffuse the light.

Throughout the space, up to the sales area, a large 11 meter cavity brushes up against the wall in order to become a display unit and light source.

On the right-hand side the wall begins with a white satin curtain which is backlit via projectors. This curtain closes off the storage space, conceals the technical installations and serves as a backdrop for the tasting area.

Moving on, the wall is then punched with niches for displaying the products. Stretching back toward the work area, it becomes a cabinet with drawers before finishing off by conforming shelves above the oven and a small loft space, where the machinery for the refrigerators is kept.

The side walls enclose the back portion of the shop with an isolated body clad in glass painted in grayish tones. This volume, which is set in the boundary between the shop and work area, behind the counter, houses the toilet and a changing room.

The platforms seem to float and the sampling tables are cantilevered surfaces above a glass prism filled with cacao beans. The display cases are either transparent glass or painted in varying shades of gray. These display cases are completely devoid of all visually extraneous elements, including metal joints and fasteners. This overall neutral treatment is abruptly and definitively interrupted with the finish of a red false ceiling, situated at a height of 2.8 meters and embracing the entire shop and work area, where it folds and drops down to form a large smoke extractor. This is the element that ties the design together and establishes a taut dialogue between all the components of the space. A stimulating, audacious and provocative dialogue, which is at the same time delicate and unified, in an attempt to create an expressive, visually alive and coherent plastic effect for the entire space.

Photographs: David Cardelús

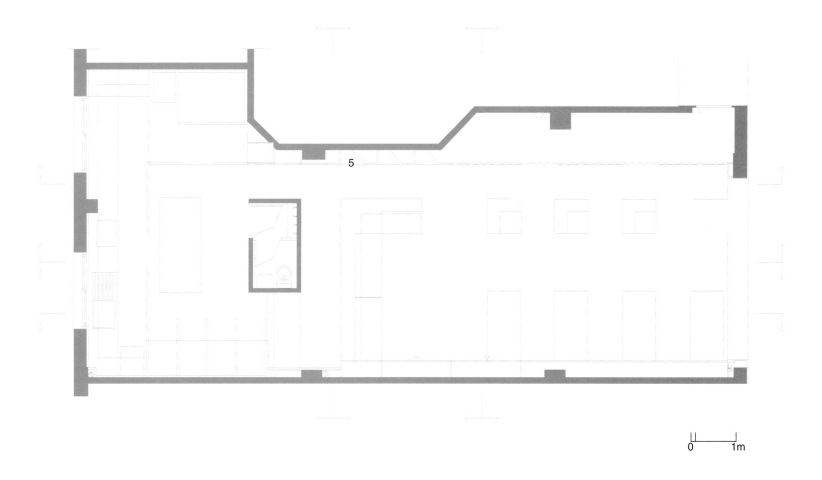

5

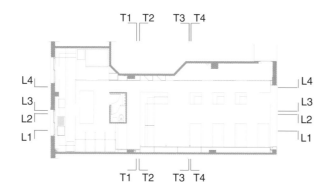

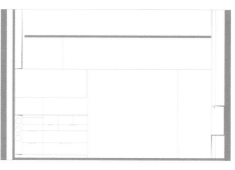

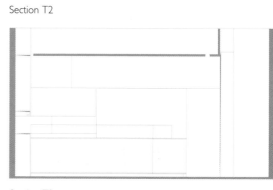

Section T1

Section T2

Section T3

Section T4

The lighting has been built into various white containers, thereby creating a lantern-like effect while highlighting the products on display. Of particular interest is the large screen providing ambient lighting, comprised of a backlit curtain. The result is a relaxing space bathed in indirect lighting set in counterpoint to the central display area of the shop, which features spotlighting built into a false ceiling.

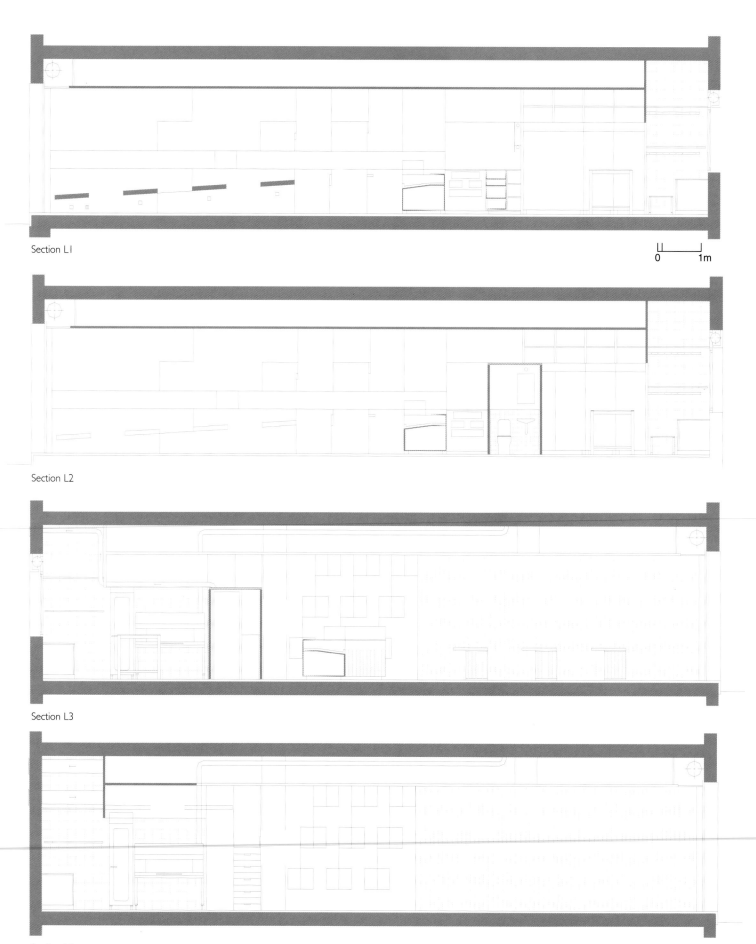

Section L1

Section L2

Section L3

Section L4

0   1m

Massimiliano Fuksas
Europark

Salzbourg, Austria

The architect gave the name "breakpoint" to the design concept of Europark SPAR, after the title of a film that tells of a passion for surfing, of a man who tries to dominate nature, the great ocean waves: in others words, a passion for freedom. This building is intended to be a territorial "landmark" that is recognizable for its commercial importance, and its strong relationship with the semi-urban context. The park is seen as a buffer zone for the surrounding residential area. In addition to its aesthetic and ecological quality, it fulfils an important practical role as a noise barrier. The project consists of two metal grid waves. It is basically an immense commercial center comprising three food halls and thirty or so shops. It has a total site area of 120,000 m² and extends over an area measuring 320 m in length and 140 m in width.

Seven hectares of parking facilities are placed under this metal grid, three thousand car-parking spaces on a red-colored surface. Great attention is paid to the distribution of different types of vehicles, lorries, private cars, cyclists and pedestrians. The exhaust fumes are eliminated by the wind and mechanical devices. The interior is designed on the fragmentation principle. The whole project is organized around three "voids", three distinct "spaces". The spaces are "interrupted" in order to admit daylight and create a pleasant atmosphere for workers on the inside. The clear horizontal arrangement of the building contrasts abruptly with the irregularity of its roofing. The joists and pillars are in reinforced steel. The facades are made of metal and glass panels that illuminate the interior and give views of the exterior. The roof is designed as a longitudinal, curved grid construction on which there is a double metal grating. The load-bearing structure is made of diagonal members that guarantee stability.

In this project, the architect worked in sections proceeding from the inside to the outside. The use of voids placed lengthwise or crosswise provides a variety of spatial sequences.

Photographs: Philippe Ruault

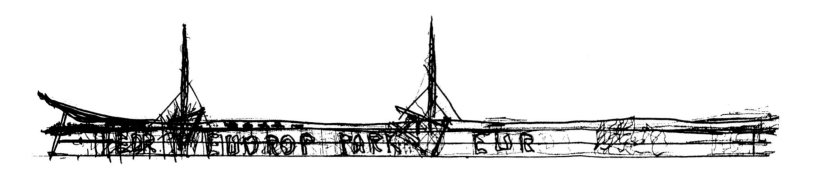

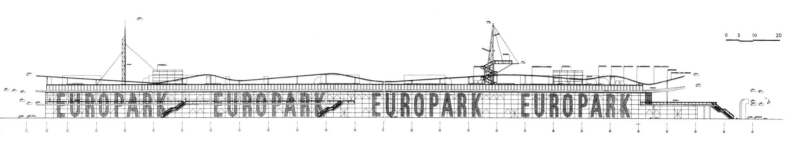

North elevation

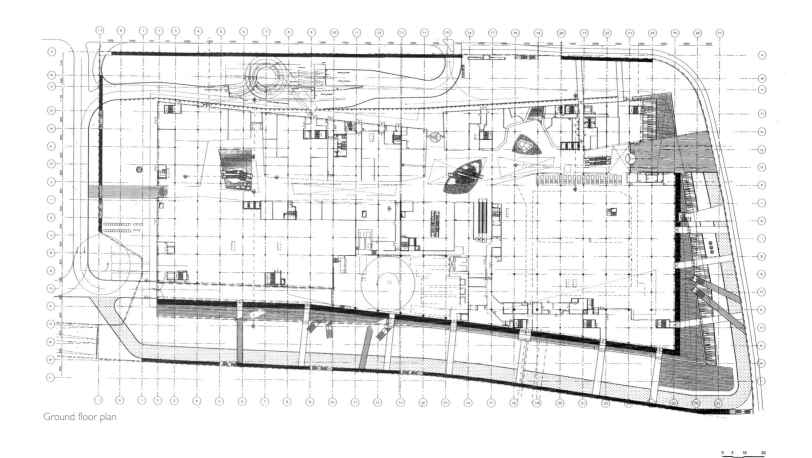

Ground floor plan

0 5 10 20

The building, which is 320 meters long by 140 meters wide, distributes its over thirty shops around three large empty spaces.

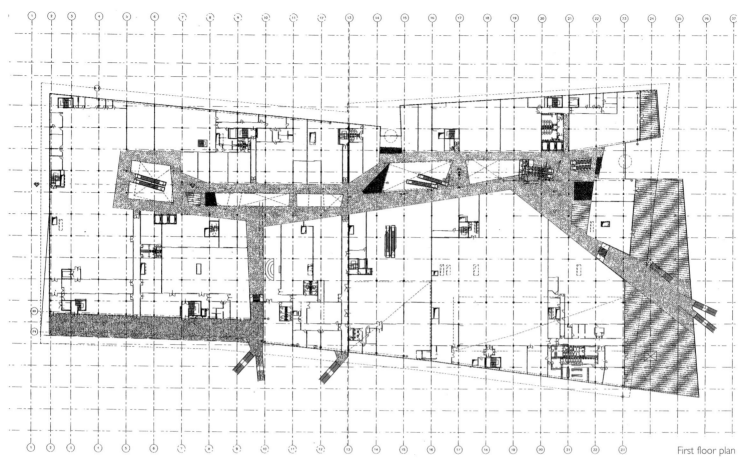

First floor plan

The outer appearance of the building features two large bright red metal wings under which the parking area is situated.

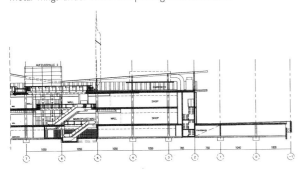

Section A1

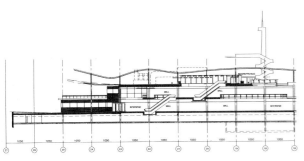

Section A2

Vincent van Duysen
Natan Boutique

Brussels, Belgium

The idea behind the Natan boutique project, in an old building in Brussels, was to create a bright but intimate atmosphere. The space is defined through white elements: load-bearing walls, pillars and beams, a mezzanine that seems to float in space, the marble staircase within an angular balustrade and the light wall of the shop window parallel to the façade. Although abstract, the minimalist white surfaces -some of them mobile- delimit the spaces where the customers, protected from the street, can try on the garments while they enjoy a view to the exterior through a horizontal opening in the wall. The street thus becomes a shop window for the customers.

The display elements match the rest of the space in color and materials, which gives uniformity to the whole and highlights the interplay of volumes and forms created between the vertical circulation space and the mezzanine.

The lighting system, spotlights fitted into a hung ceiling and perimeter lighting, help to enhance the brightness of the boutique. The hung ceiling does not touch the wall, and, as if suspended in the air, it momentarily breaks the uniformity of the space. This arrangement forms part of the interplay of volumes and geometries of the design: lines that cut through each other, juxtaposition and overlapping of bodies. The mezzanine highlights the vertical dimension of the space and creates an interplay of heights on the ground floor. Windows with black shutters on the outside and white ones on the inside soften the impact of the entrance to the boutique and use the metaphor of color to show the contrast between the hustle and bustle of the street and the clear peacefulness of this space. The interior is thus disconnected from the urban environment and the starring role is given to the garments.

Photographs: Alberto Piovano

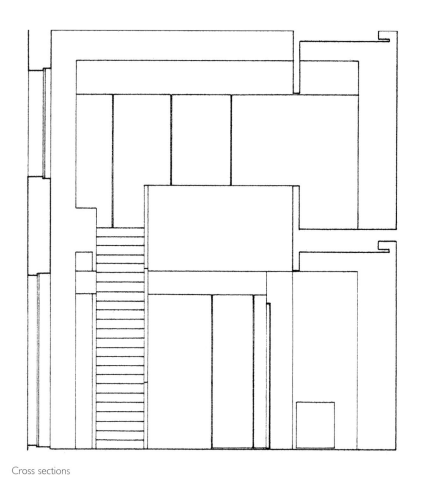

Cross sections

153

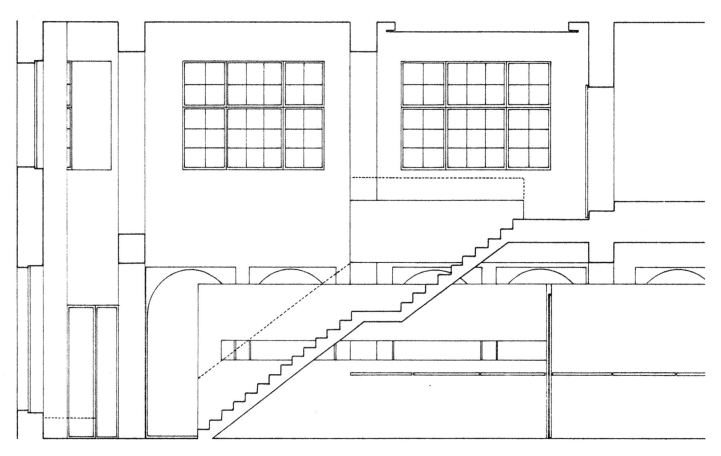

Longitudinal section

The location of the building that houses the boutique, at the corner of two streets, had a decisive influence on the design concept. The aim was to isolate the boutique by giving it a high degree of autonomy in order to prevent the urban environment from invading the interior space.

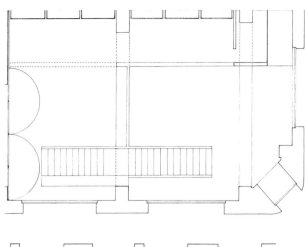

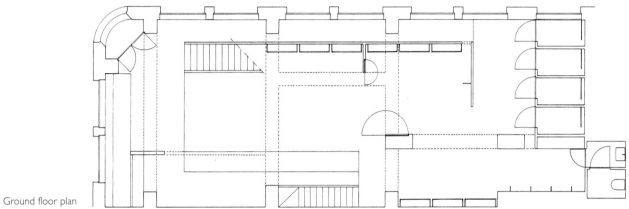

Ground floor plan

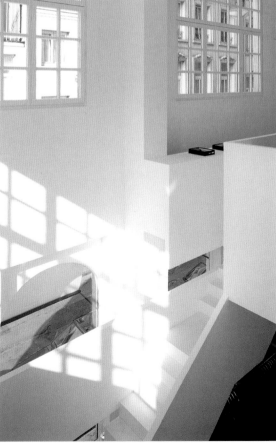

155

Steven Holl + Vito Acconci
Storefront for Art & Architecture

New York, USA

In 1992, Steven Holl and the artist Vito Acconci were commissioned as a collaborative team to renovate the aging facade of the Storefront for Art and Architecture, one of the few galleries dedicated to the exhibition of young architects in New York City. The Storefront project is the second collaborative effort by Holl and Acconci; their first work together was a 1988 urban plan for a growing arts community in downtown Washington D.C. sponsored by the Pennsylvania Avenue Development Corporation.

The Storefront for Art and Architecture is situated on the corner of a block that marks the intersection of three distinct neighborhoods: Chinatown, Little Italy and Soho. The gallery itself is a limited, narrow wedge with a triangulated exhibition interior, such that the most dominant structure for the Storefront for Art and Architecture is the building's long facade. In fact, the history of exhibitions at the gallery was marked in the various cuts and layers of paint which exhibiting architects had imposed on and through this once-uniform surface.

Drawing from this history, neither Acconci nor Holl were interested in the permanence of the facade or the idea of a static gallery space. Seeking to introduce improbability and to puncture the facade, Acconci and Holl challenged this symbolic border, which underlines the exclusivity of the art world, where only those on the inside belong. Using a hybrid material comprised of concrete mixed with recycled fibers, Holl and Acconci inserted a series of hinged panels arranged in a puzzle-like configuration. When the panels are locked in their open position, the facade dissolves and the interior space of the gallery expands out onto the sidewalk. If the function of a facade is to create a division separating the inside from the outside space, this new facade, in the words of director Kyong Park is "no wall, no barrier, no inside, no outside, no space, no building, no place, no institution, no art, no architecture, no Acconci, no Holl, no storefront."

Photographs: Paul Warchol

Floor plan

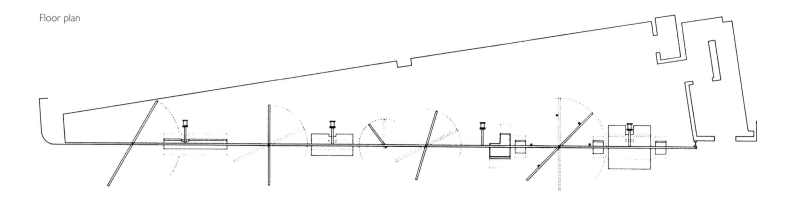

Due to the dimensions of the site, the fundamental component through which
the project was developed is undoubtedly the long, extensive street facade.

The gallery, which was designed for exhibiting the work of young architects, occupies a narrow, triangular, wedge-shaped corner site.

When the pivoting elements are fully opened, the limited indoor space projects street wards. By means of this ingenious system, the architect succeeds in melting the facade away and endowing the premises with more space.

Ian Ritchie Architects
Leipzig Neue Messe Glass Halls

Leipzig, Germany

Having won an international competition in 1992, Professor Marg invited Ian Ritchie Architects to collaborate with him, along with IPP Ingenieurbüro and HL-Technik, in the design and realization of the huge glass winter garden which is the centerpiece of the new Leipzig International Exhibition Center. The glass hall is 238 m long, 80 m wide, and 28 m high at the apex, and includes four separate single-story stone faced buildings providing catering, shopping & cloakroom facilities. A central work area has been designated to provide reception, relaxation and meeting area for conference delegates. Six bridges run through and across the hall 5 m above the main floor level. They are enclosed in curved glass linking the main hall with the exhibition halls and conference center. A further bridge links it with the other entrance pavilion across a water landscape.

The building sought to achieve simplicity with economy, allowing it to exist as a filigree shell within the central landscape of the site. The vaulted structured is composed of an external orthogonal single layer grid shell of uniform-diameter tube stiffened by primary arches of 25 m diameter. The envelope is composed of low-iron PPG starfire laminated glass panels measuring 1.5 x 3.125 m, suspended 0.5 m below the grid shell, and includes discreet perimeter ventilation/smoke extract "butterfly" openings at high level. Entrances are located in both end walls.

Environmental control is achieved in summer through the opening vents. In exceptionally hot periods de-ionized water is run from the apex over the glass vault. Underfloor heating maintains a minimum internal temperature of 8°C at 2 m above ground level, with perimeter heating counteracting downdraughts and minimizing condensation.

Photographs: Jocelyne Van Den Bossche

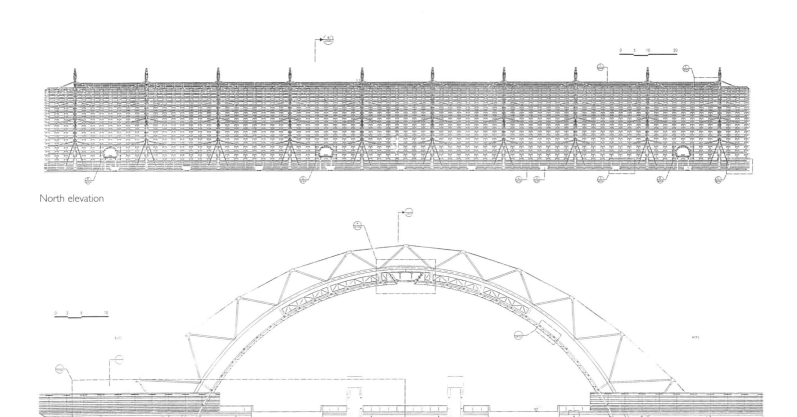

North elevation

Cross section

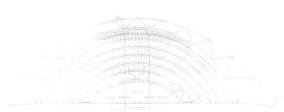

West elevation

The dimensions of the large winter garden built entirely of glass and steel are impressive: 238 meters long, 80 meters wide and 28 meters high at the highest point. The simplicity and economy of the materials do not detract from the majestic result.

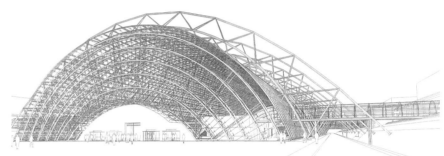

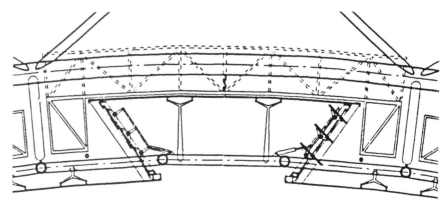

Detail of ventilation duct

Ramon Esteve
Farrutx Palma

Palma de Mallorca, Spain

This project is a shop for a line of shoes in the city of Palma, Majorca. The premises not only had to house a store but also to act as the flagship of the company, representing its values. The brief was to restore commercial premises located in a building with historical value in the Passeig des Born, a shopping area of Palma. The ground plan was originally rectangular, a free container of flat walls and right angles that the architect respected, treating the walls with affection and giving back to them the dignity of their nakedness.

The façade was restored, the destroyed part reconstructed from molds taken from the symmetrical side using the same type of stone as the original and the same manual process.

Access from the street is through the only opening in the façade, which becomes both entrance and window. The whole area of the shop is thus transformed into an immense display for the products, which can be seen from the street through a 2 cm thick glass door weighing almost 250 kg. Worked by a movement sensor, a mechanism triggers the silent motor to slide the heavy glass sheet, which is absorbed by the threshold as though it were a thin membrane. At the back, three panes of translucent glass are illuminated from the rear. Fitted without frames, clean from top to bottom, housed simply in the stone of the floor and the plaster of the ceiling, they give the sensation that the space extends beyond the limits of the premises. The furniture forms an integral part of the architecture of the shop, consisting of freestanding elements, solid 12-centimeter-thick slabs of polished Bateig stone that rest on a cross made of the same material. Benches divide the store into sub-spaces, aligning everything for pure tranquility. Organizing the usual elements of a shop within the space, creating an atmosphere that inspires contemplation and marrying the building tradition with the latest technological innovations is an exercise in synthesis. Clearing a wall of molding and skirting is a declaration of principles. Controlling the light by illuminating each corner without leaving a bulb or spotlight visible is a contained homage to architecture, removing anything that is not essential.

Photographs: contributed by the architects

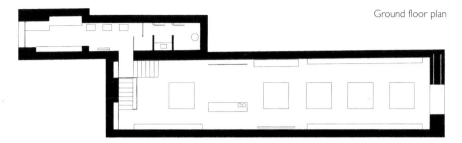

Ground floor plan

The layout of the display elements marks the different sub-spaces of the store. Austerity and chromatic restraint guided the choice of materials: benches and paving of Bateig sandstone, Wengué wood furniture and suspended shelves and accessories of stainless steel with a burnished finish.

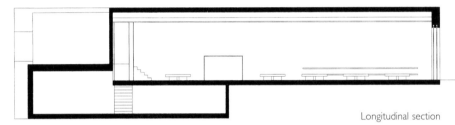

Longitudinal section

Studio Baciocchi
Miu Miu

Milan, Italy

The impact of the Miu Miu boutique in its environment, the Corso Venezia of Milan, immediately defines the rigorous linear philosophy of the architectural project: the shop window opens up in a façade clad with gray cement slabs, framing the geometries and forms of an interior space of 400 m^2 developed horizontally.

Roberto Baciochi has created large volumes divided by panels that define the different display areas and always leave open spaces at intersection points with the walls and ceiling. Steps and a ramp provide easy access to the different levels of the store. The result is a space of great unity, free of superfluous decorative elements.

The use of materials reflects a desire for contrast rather than homogeneity or balance. Gray cement has been used for the floor and the counter, while polished aluminum is reserved for the display units -shelves, cabinets and hangers- and for the benches, which are consoles covered by leather cushions and attached to the canvas-lined walls. The walls and ceiling are plastered in white, while the color red defines the panels that divide the space and serve as a frame for the garments on display. The interior of the display units is also painted red. This color is only used on certain surfaces, marking elements of special relevance and contributing a dynamic feel to the space. The display models hang from the ceiling and are illuminated at the lower part of the bust. The white-plastered fitting rooms have etched glass doors. Lights fitted into longitudinal slashes in the ceiling illuminate the space and enhance the quality of the garments. The result is a unique and stimulating atmosphere, the perfect support for the Miu Miu line.

Photographs: Alberto Piovano

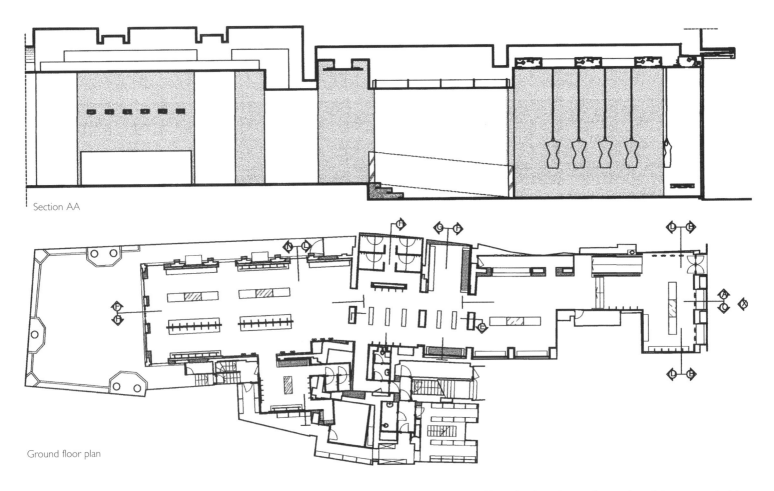

Section AA

Ground floor plan

Steps and a ramp have been used to connect the different levels of the long, deep floor and give the space a dynamic feel.

Color plays a major role in this project. The red and gray form a vibrant palette that serves as a backdrop to the garments on display and defines the route through the different spaces of the boutique.

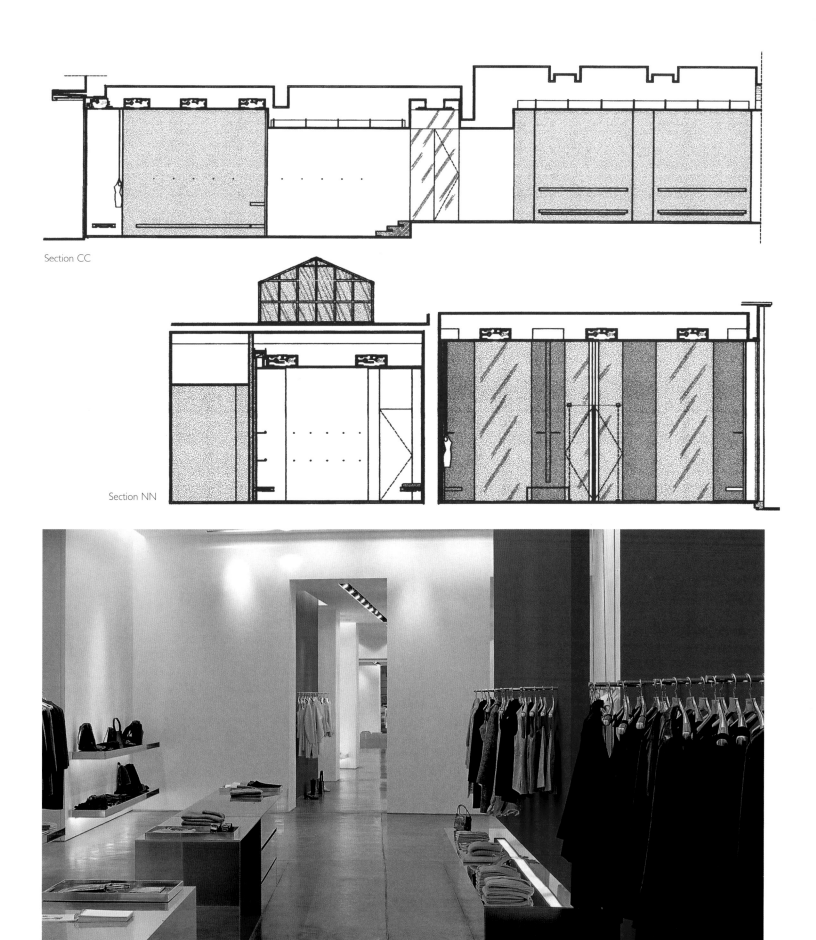

Section CC

Section NN

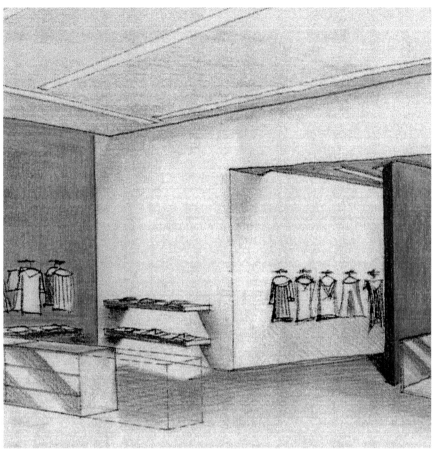

Sergio Calatroni
Copy Center

Shizuoka, Japan

The 66 m² premises located in a shopping mall have become a focus of attention, an advertisement and the representative image of this copy service company. The scheme is integrated in mall elements, thus creating a sensation of greater space. The premises function as a shop window presenting the work that goes on inside it.

The scheme is developed through a startling interplay of lights, textures and colors that attract the attention of potential customers. The architect used transparent and reflective materials such as glass, metal, mirrors and colored Plexiglas. Most of the furniture is painted in opaque gold.

The purity of forms and the simplicity of the walls collaborate with the materials to enhance the intensity of the colors, which form an integral part of the design. The architect thus uses the interplay of light and color as a major element of the design.

Photographs: Sergio Calatroni

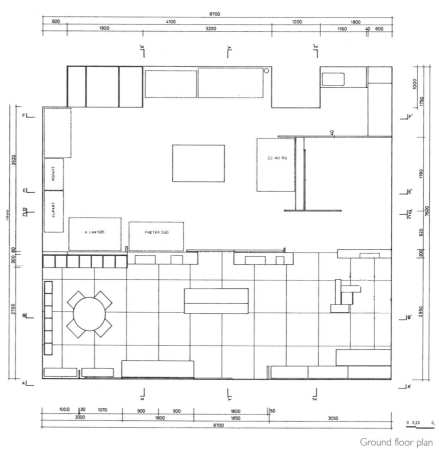

Ground floor plan

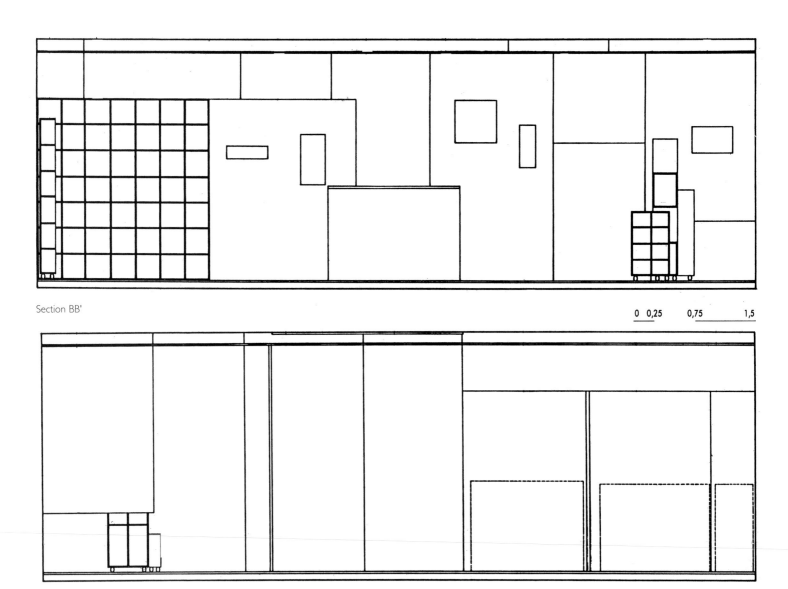

Section BB'

0 0,25   0,75   1,5

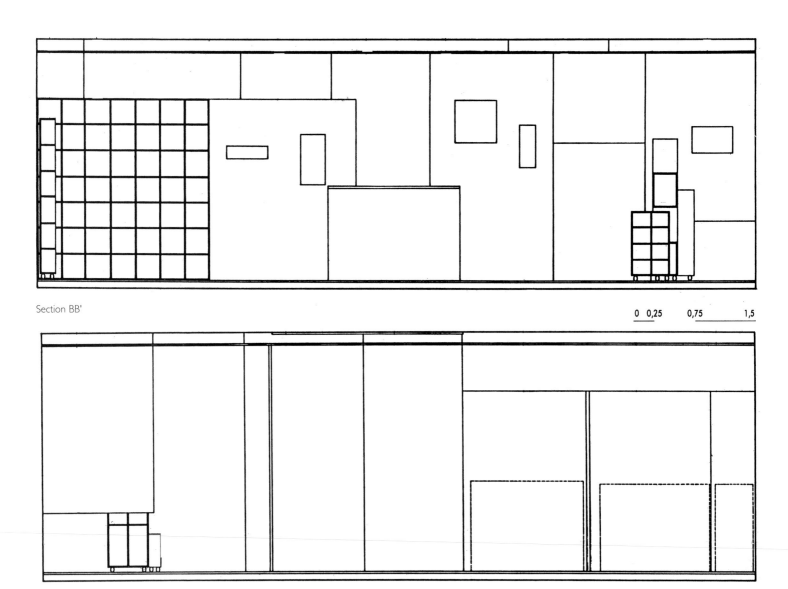

Section CC'

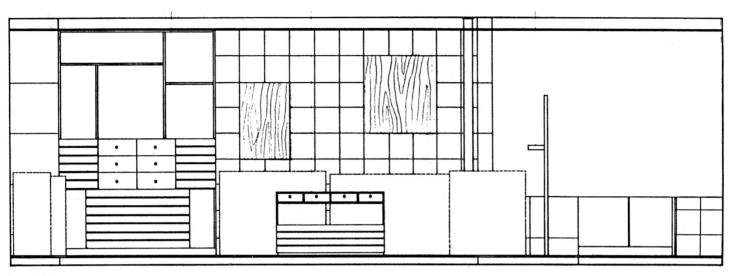

Section EE'

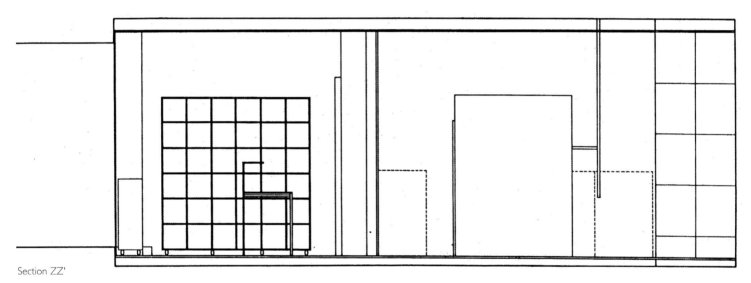

Section ZZ'

Sage Wimer Coombe
Janovic Plaza

New York City, USA

In the renovated space of the Janovic Plaza paint store, light plays a fundamental role: it is an essential element for choosing a certain shade of paint, a wallpaper or a curtain.

Color is the other factor that defines the project. Following these guidelines, Sage Wimer Coombe designed a shop in which illustrations and famous quotes about color and the home entertain and inspire customers.

The shop has been paved with white terrazzo tiles inlaid with small fragments of colored glass. This choice of floor unifies the space and provides a background on which the colors and more complex designs can coexist. The terrazzo is repeated for the tops of the tables distributed around the whole store. Large patches of paint unify the irregular design of the columns. Between the paint section and the home decoration section, a space is devoted to color selection. This environment of deliberately neutral tones uses different types of light sources (incandescent lamps, fluorescent lamps, and different types of simulated natural light) so that customers can imagine the different possibilities of lighting that can be used in a house.

The oval molding placed over the wall conceals a lamp and illuminates the atmosphere in cavetto. Around this molding is a quote from Paul Klee: "Painting well is no more than this: putting the right color in the right place". In the section devoted to upholstery, tables with terrazzo tops allow customers to choose in comfort. Six round lights illuminate this atmosphere surrounded by a soffit painted a deep purple and rich yellow on which illuminated frames display images of great rooms.

Photographs: Michael Moran

Ground floor plan

1. Residential building lobby
2. Column
3. Store entry
4. Service entry
5. Cash desk
6. Window display
7. Display wall
8. Paint department
9. Color selection room
10. Sliding window treatment display
11. Interior design center
12. Emergency exit

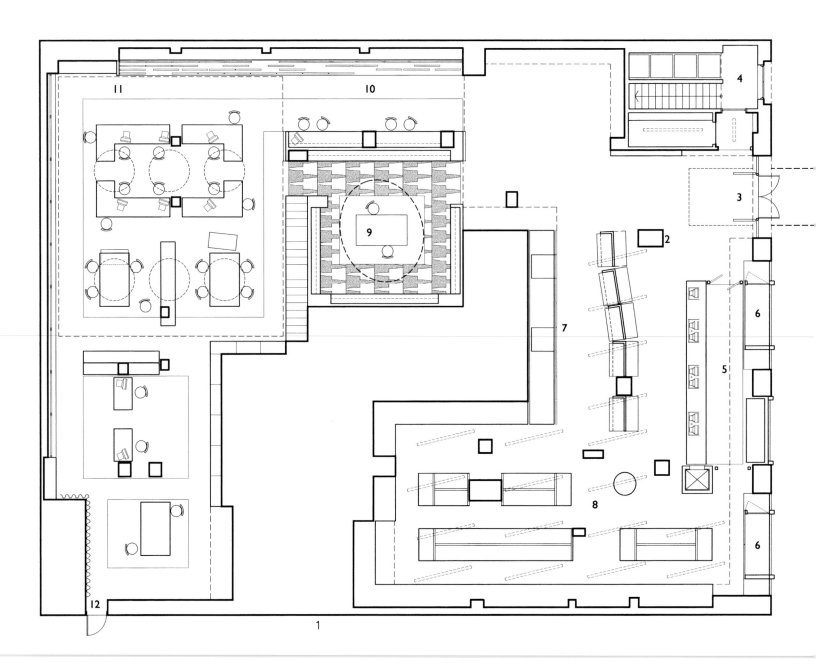

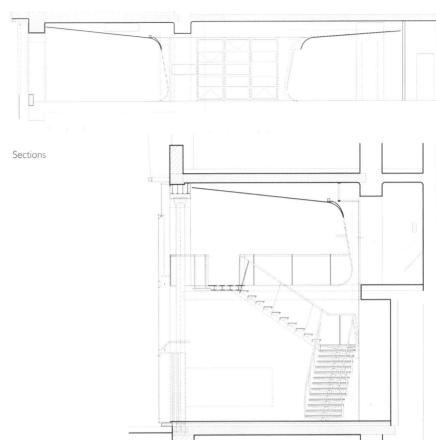

Sections

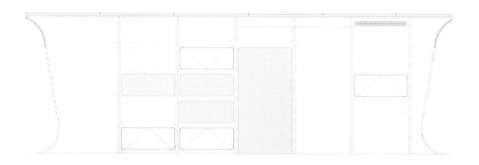

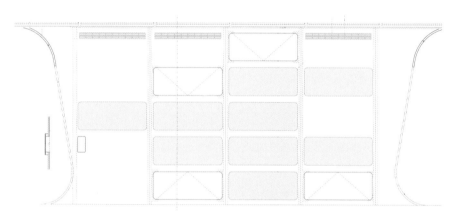

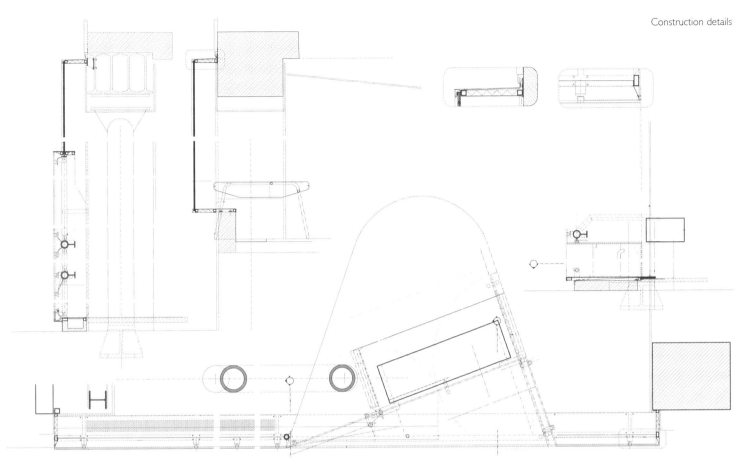

Maria Canosa
Solanes O'Clock

Reus, Spain

The Project called for the adaptation of a centrally-located, ground floor shop with an open-plan layout of 80 m² of available space. The project needed to meet the basic requirement of functionality: all of the products (a mid-range brand of jewelry and watches) should be on display at once. The clients also requested a youthful design concept, yet one that would not exclude the rest of the public.

The program's general organization revolves around a central axis (its origin coinciding with the entrance vestibule) that distributes the space destined for the public, thereby delimiting the spaces reserved exclusively for internal use. In this way three circulation areas have been created and the interior has become a large opaque box with only the necessary support to enable it to function.

The objects on display are integrated into the side walls, with watches on one side and jewelry on the other. Each display space has individual lighting to draw attention.

The materials chosen are simple and are often used in works with a reduced budget. Their layout and color provides an image of the whole where all the elements are integrated through the use of the same language.

The external shell has been built from MDF, along with all of the furnishings incorporated into the shop. In certain places there are transparent glass enclosures and mirror cladding as well as stratified board. Maple wood brings together all of the elements that shape the area for attending to the public, and methacrylate allows the light to shine through it.

Photographs: Jordi Canosa

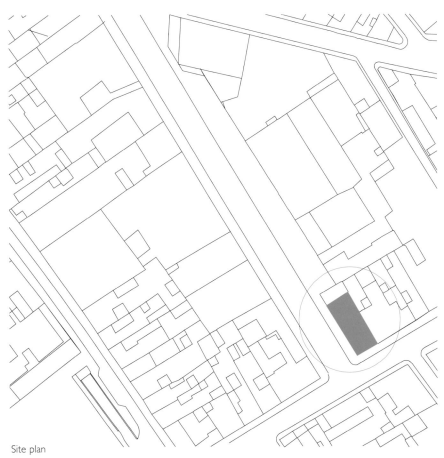

Site plan

Synthetic stone appears in the composition of the entrance façade, highlighting the shop windows situated on each side of the entrance, and extends to the interior as a general cladding of the vestibule to create a neutral space, in contrast to the bold colors of the interior.

Façades

solanes o'clock

solanes o'clock

0   1   2m

192

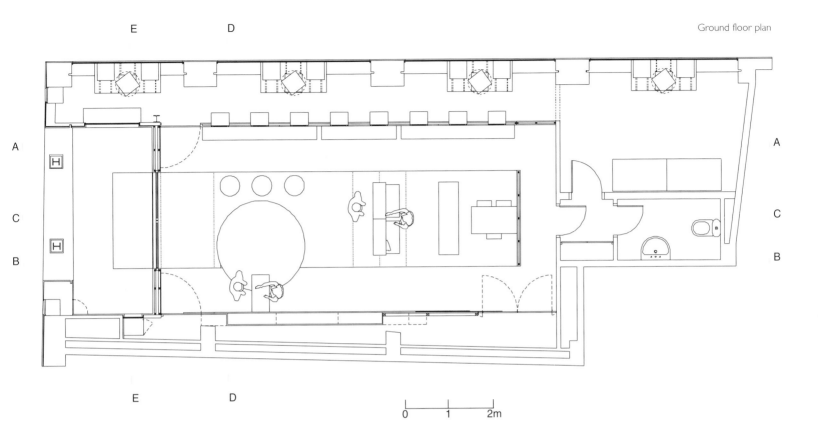

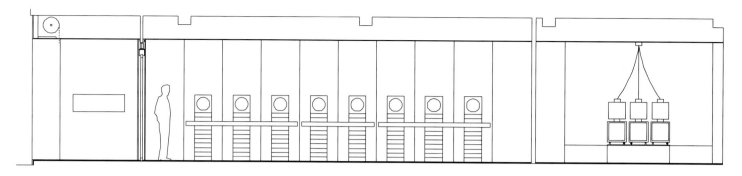

Section A-A

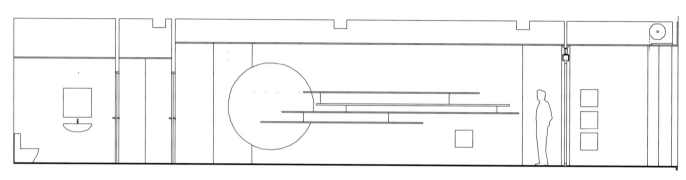

Section B-B

0   1   2m

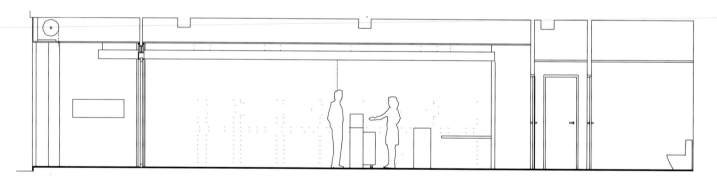

Section C-C

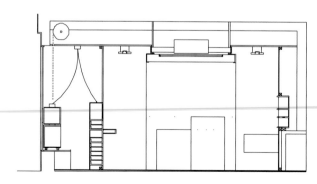

Section D-D

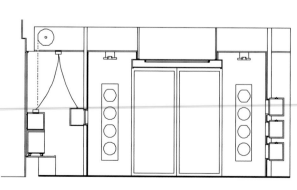

Section E-E

Neil M. Denari Architects, Inc.
I. a. Eyeworks Store

Los Angeles, USA

For this 1150 ft^2 store located on Beverly Blvd., the clients' demand was based on a unique relationship between the conventions of commercial retail practice (the temporal) and the stability (the atemporal) of architecture more often associated with institutional or public work.

As a form of new "spatial identity", the store finds its idea at the moment where the fixity of architecture and the seasonal change of new lines of glasses come together. Quite often seen to be at odds with one another, architecture's slowness has been posited as the antidote to fashion. Indeed, while fashion is intentionally based on quick stylistic shifts, the clients asked that the design of the store resist not the ephemerality of fashion, but rather resist the fashion of architecture without recourse to minimalism or lack of expression.

In working with the basic parameters of store design, such as the demand for transparency from the street, the design shapes space and movement through a continuous suspended surface. This gaseous blue surface performs many functions: perforated ceiling plane, window display, bench, shelving unit, and sales counter.

By merging the functional demand with the formal ambitions of continuity, architecture and eyeglasses fuse as a coordinated design. In between the fixity of the space and the products on sale, a group of furniture elements, all on wheels and designed by NMDA, acts as a mediator of scale and movement.

Photographs: Benny Chan / Fotoworks

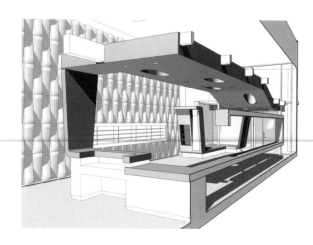

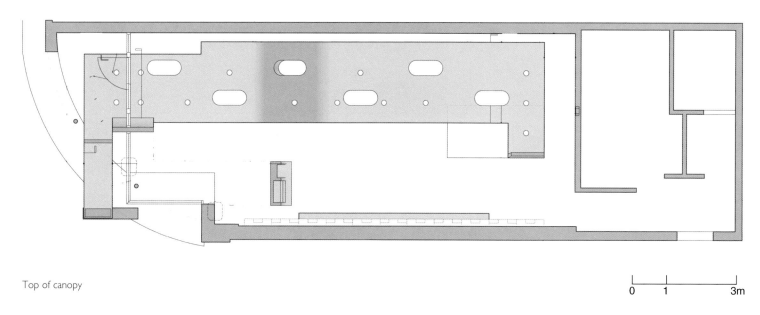

Top of canopy

```
0    1         3m
```

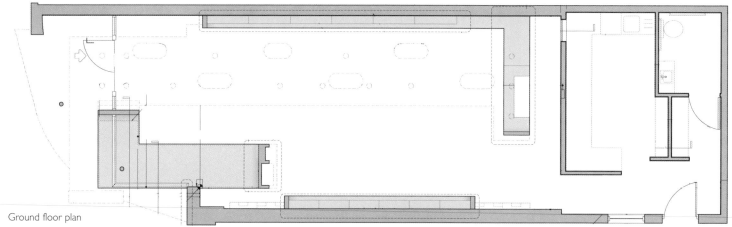

Ground floor plan

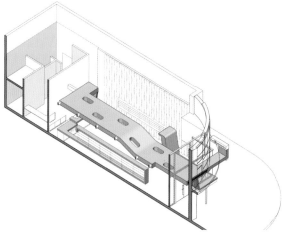

A wall consisting of 56 vacuum-formed polystyrene panels, designed by the artist Jim Isermann, fills the entire west wall of the store. The repetitive pattern of the panels is the graphic field against which the rest of the store may be perceived. The display cabinets and sales desk are composed of MDF with high preparation polyurethane paint, while the ceiling is clad in painted gypsum wallboard.

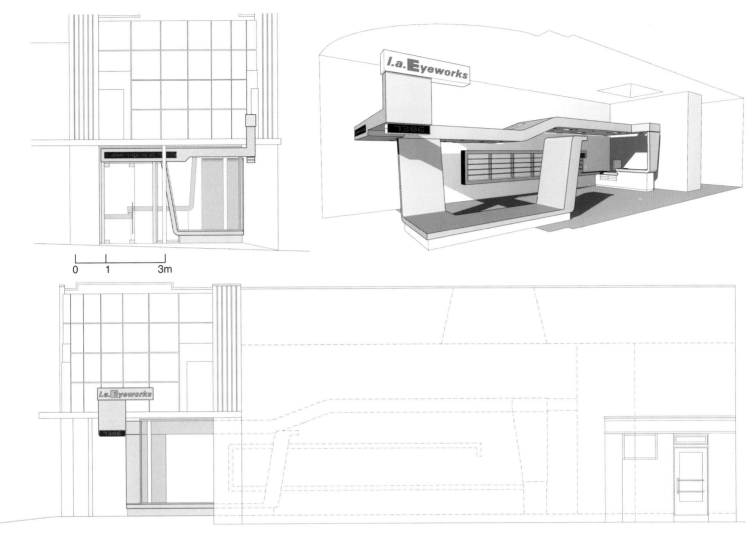

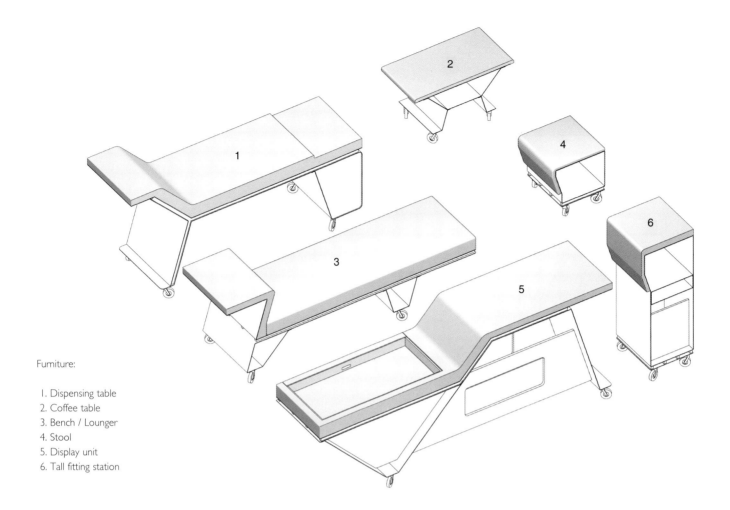

Furniture:

1. Dispensing table
2. Coffee table
3. Bench / Lounger
4. Stool
5. Display unit
6. Tall fitting station

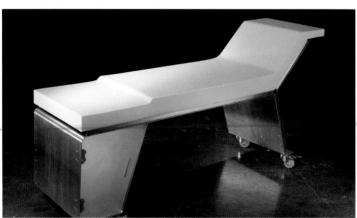

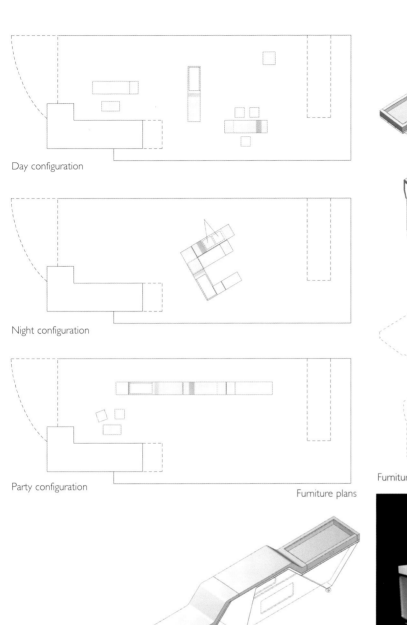

Day configuration

Night configuration

Party configuration

Furniture plans

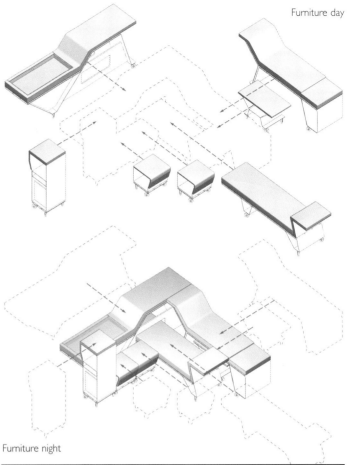

Furniture day

Furniture night

Furniture party

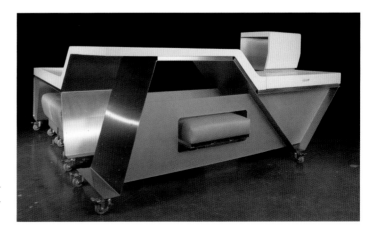

Denari custom designed the furniture with the assistance of a workshop with experience in aerospace technolgy, where the folded 3 mm stainless steel plates were laser-cut to precision. The surfaces are sanded Corian.

204

Phillipe Starck
Asia de Cuba

London, UK

Located in the stylish St. Martin's Lane Hotel in the heart of London's Convent Garden, this vibrant restaurant and bar serves an unusual fusion of Asian and Latino food. The entire space covers two levels and accommodates around 165 customers.

At the entrance to the Rum Bar -one of the few overt references to Cuban culture- guests find themselves before a series of tall, slender steel tables with just enough room on the surface for a couple of drinks. These were custom designed for the project by Starck, as were the upholstered banquettes in the restarant, set against white walls.

Neutral elements such as a maple floor and Scandinavian-style laminate chairs, featuring back slipcovers with insets of Italian lace, are offset by the more dramatic presence of rows of massive columns, each of displaying a different motif.

More than mere static and functional supports, these columns become a central element of the design. Shelves arranged around their perimeter are overflowing with black and white photographs, flowerpots filled with plants or fresh flowers, or books on geography and history. Others may be upholstered in quilted cotton or clad in iridescent silk. One is simply covered in blackboard paint for customers to freely draw on.

Unadorned hanging lightbulbs are a simple lighting solution which serve as a counterpoint to the visually-heavy volume of the columns. The overall atmosphere is unique and somewhat surreal, but not fixed: in adhering to the desire to be able to change the look of this space on a regular basis, the open design scheme is intended to provide endless options for rearranging and restructuring.

Photographs: Mihail Moldoveano

At the entrance to the Rum Bar -one of the few overt references to Cuban culture- guests find themselves before a series of tall, slender steel tables with just enough room on the surface for a couple of drinks.

Fabio Novembre
Shu Café

Milano, Italy

Steel, molded glass, shattered glass, glass punctured by bullets, fiber optics systems and enlarged circuit boards are just some of the inventive elements which set this project apart as a thoroughly modern, highly uninhibited design.

An imposing oval-shaped bar, with under-lit steps radiating outward and upwards toward the ceiling, greets patrons as they enter from the one of the corners of the bar. A velvet curtain separates the bar area from the restaurant and also softens the cold feel of the rest of the materials.

In the restaurant, two giant fore-arms sprout from the ground and support the false ceiling. The original columns have been incorporated within these giant sculptures of glass resin clad in gold leaf. The green enamel false ceiling slopes toward the bar on the back wall, playing a trick on the eye and making the room seem longer than it is. Light boxes designed like the internal circuits of a computer are arranged along the ceiling in a pattern also recalling a circuit board.

The walls in the restaurant are composed of tiny, shimmering black mosaic tiles. Along one lateral wall is the "St. Valentine's wall", made with armored glass slabs perforated by bullet holes and illuminated on its profile.

The bar is made with sheets of shattered glass, back-lit by optical fibers and framed in steel.

Photographs: Alberto Ferrero

Floor plan

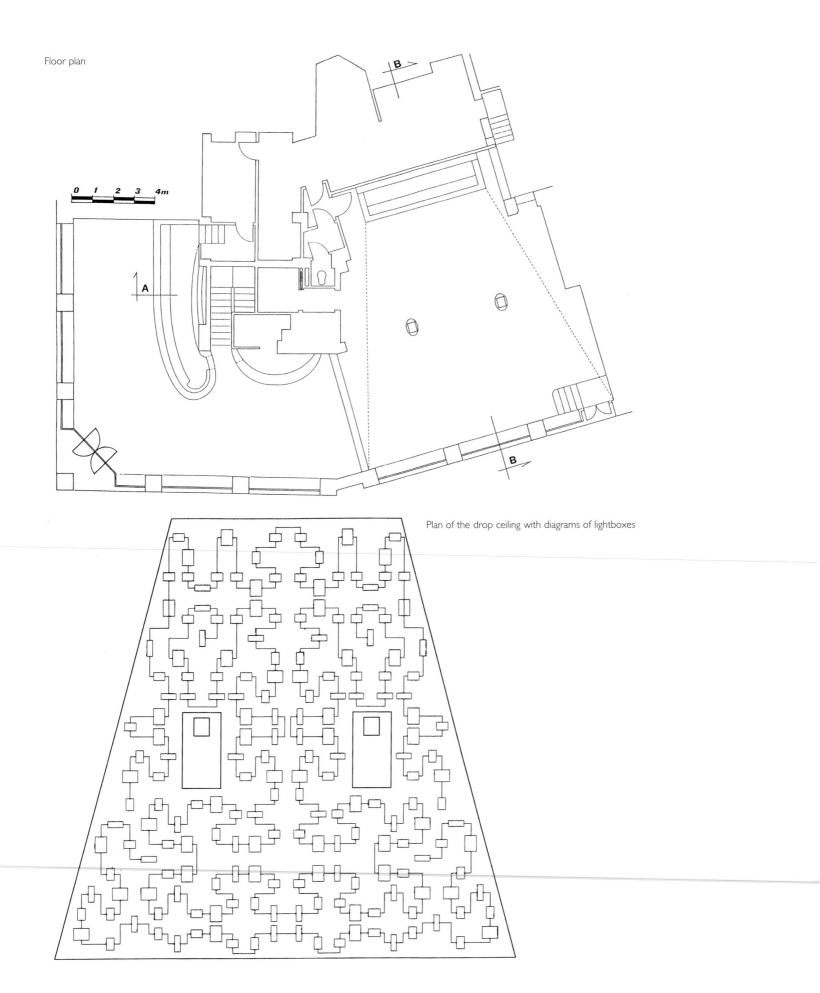

0 1 2 3 4m

A

B

B

Plan of the drop ceiling with diagrams of lightboxes

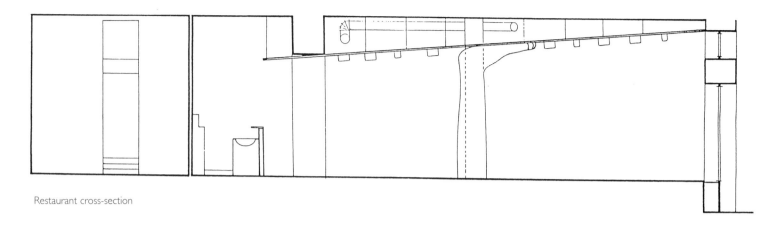

Restaurant cross-section

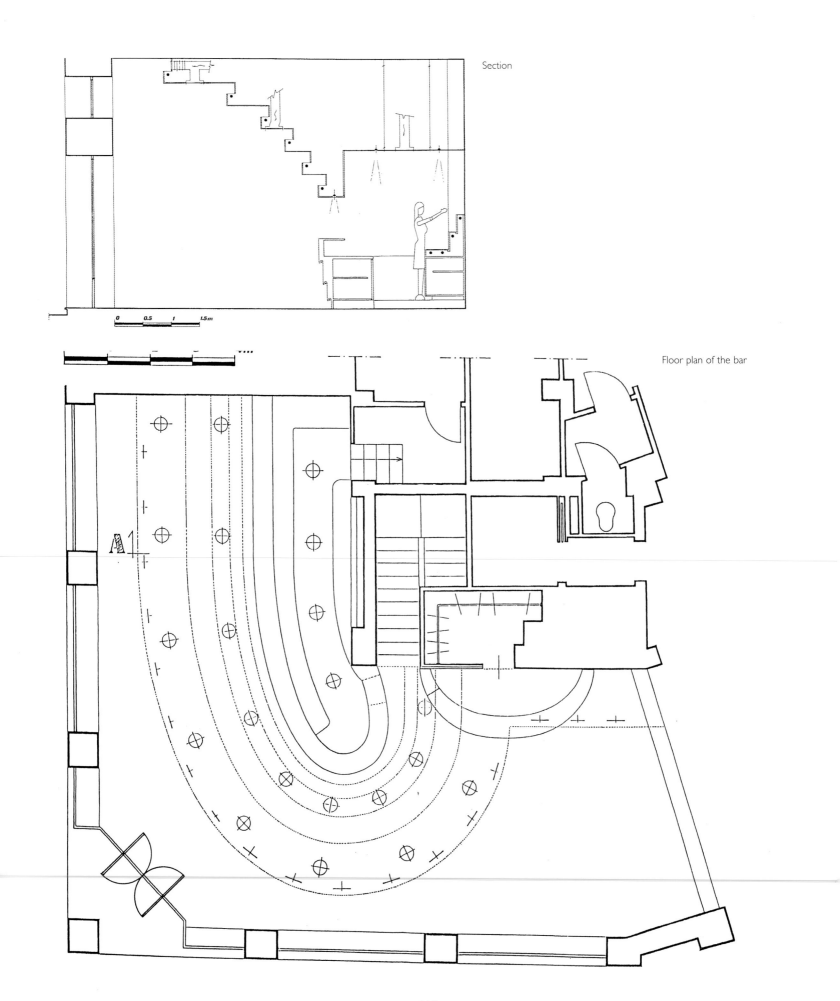

Section

Floor plan of the bar

0   0.5   1   1.5 m

A1

214

215

Diller + Scofidio
The Brasserie

New York City, USA

The prospect of redesigning one of New York's legendary restaurants in one of the world's most distinguished modernist buildings, Mies van der Rohe's Seagram building, was as inviting as it was daunting.

The design emphasizes the social aspects of dining, adding a new dimension to the phrase "making an entrance". A sensor in the revolving entry door triggers a video snapshot that is added to a continuously changing display of 15 LCD monitors over the bar, thereby announcing patrons before they have entered the main space. The descent into the main dining room (several feet below street level), is theatricized: a glass-walled stairway of unusually gradual proportions prolongs the descent of arriving guests.

After removing all traces of the previous interior (most of which had been destroyed by fire) the rough concrete surfaces of the original space have been relined with new skins of wood, terrazzo, tile and glass. The madrone wood floor peels up at the edges while the pearwood ceiling curves down and is molded to form a long bench running the length of the room. A slender space flanking the main dining area, opposite the bar, is sliced into private booths by a series of tall, upholstered slabs tipped up on end and propped on steel legs.

In the rear dining room, a 48-foot-long glass wall leans against a perimeter wall and sheaths a display of artifacts. The lenticular glass teases vision by blurring all but perpendicular views. The equation between glass and fragility is exploited: the tipped glass wall supports 24 seated diners along its length. Also in the rear dining room, 25mm pear-veneered plywood elements peel away from the plaster ceiling and wall to become free-floating, illuminated partitions.

Photographs: Michael Moran

Second dining room

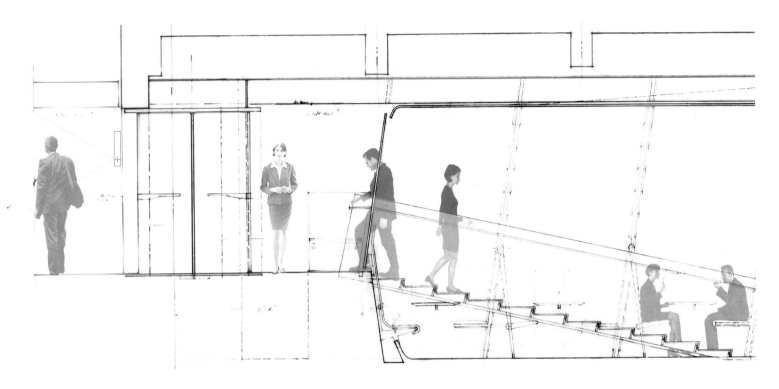

Staircase section

The madrone wood floor peels up at the edges while the pearwood ceiling curves down to form a long bench running the length of the room. The narrow space opposite the bar is divided into private booths by tall, upholstered slabs tipped on end and supported by steel legs.

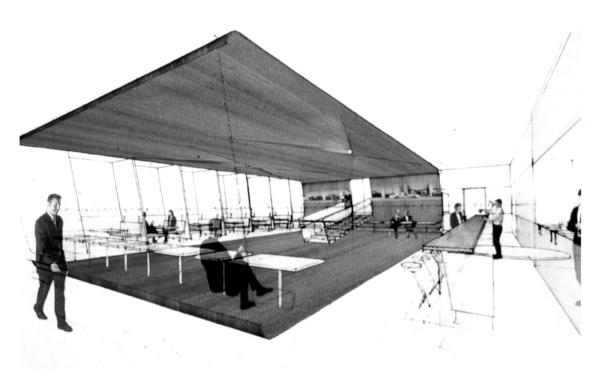

Antonello Boschi
Bar-Restaurant "L'Arca"

Follonica, Italy

The first impression of this bar/restaurant, perched on a wooden gangway jutting out over the water, can be misleading The structure is simple enough: a single-story rectangle clad in dark wood and somehow reminiscent of a seaman's bar on some desolate wharf. Closer inspection, however, reveals a subtle combination of sleek design elements, such as stainless steel and ground glass, and the warmth of wood. The interior design consciously seeks a streamlined look, while emulating the early ocean-liners of the 1930s.

Just past the entrance door, with its two round windows like portholes, is the bar area. Here, two tapered pilasters covered in stainless steel contrast with the cherry wood panels that line the walls. Sheets of stainless steel mesh line the bar, behind which are simple ground glass shelves and back-lit wooden panels.

A row of round lights embedded in the floor leads to the dining room, which is opened up to include an outdoor terrace in the warmer months. The choice of materials corresponds to their usage and role. Hence the walls are lined with wood to absorb sound in the space set aside for live music. Stainless steel is used in the dining room for its resistance to daily use.

Particular care has been taken with the lighting. The only sources of light in the bar are two delicate rows of small, evenly-spaced round lights in the wood paneling and a number of round lights embedded into the ceiling and floor. In the concert area a mixture of bright halogen lighting and hanging lamps creates a unique atmosphere. In the dining room, the tables are illuminated by a large custom-made lamp with an imaginative motif recalling either a mass of cumulous clouds or a coral reef. In the bathroom, a cluster of tiny lights set into a blue ceiling are reflected on the surrounding walls, creating the effect of a starry sky.

Photographs: Alessandro Ciampi

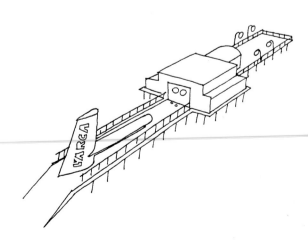

222

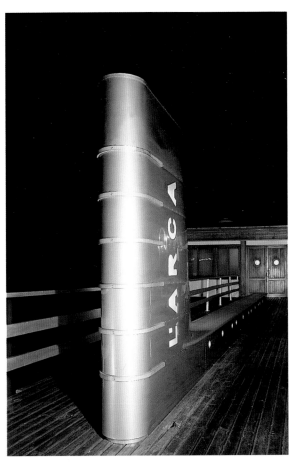

Cherry wood panels were chosen for the interior flooring and wall cladding to add warmth and absorb sound. The custom designed lamp in the dining area is meant to evoke a mass of clouds.

The aluminum chairs and tables are light and easy to stow, making it possible to quickly convert the seating area into a dance floor.

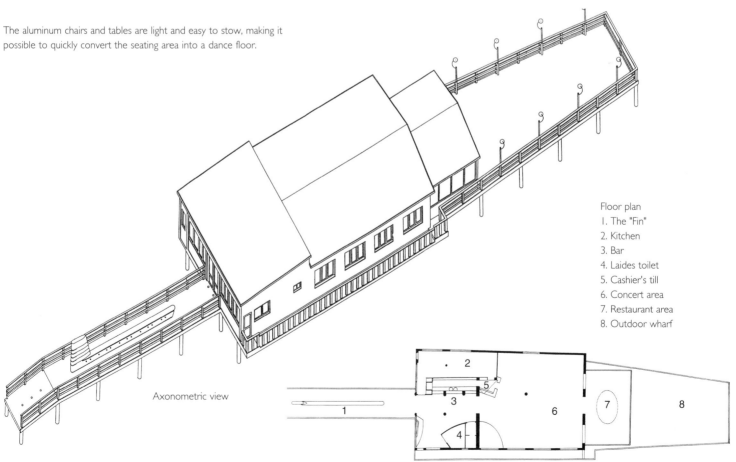

Axonometric view

Floor plan
1. The "Fin"
2. Kitchen
3. Bar
4. Laides toilet
5. Cashier's till
6. Concert area
7. Restaurant area
8. Outdoor wharf

Juha Ilonen
Oasis Restaurant

Helsinki, Finland

This restaurant forms part of an ambitious project to revamp Helsinki's dock area and, as a consequence of the location, its architecture was directly inspired by the nearby dockside buildings, cranes and ships.

All of the public spaces in this restaurant have been oriented toward the west in order to take advantage of views of the harbor basin. A street terrace with seating for 120 patrons borders a bustling promenade along the Helsinki waterfront.

The entrance to the restaurant is located under a glass-encased spiral staircase, which leads to the roof terrace. The dining room of the restaurant and the roof terrace (with seating capacity for 120 people) above it are elongated and narrow, thereby providing views of the harbor for all of the guests seated here. The elongated shape of the restaurant's interior, combined with the basin, creates an ever-changing mural painting: the evening sun reflects off the water and glimmers on the long rear wall of the restaurant.

While the primary material used in the building is steel in various forms -either galvanized or painted dark gray- translucent glass blocks dominate the street side of the building. The upper part of the window in the main dining room is of frosted glass, which diffuses the light and cuts down on glare. The cold, metal feel of the spiral staircase will be softened in time when creepers grow over the steel mesh screen.

On the whole, the steely, black architectural vocabulary of the building consciously follows the spirit of the magnificent transatlantic passenger ships of the early 1900s, the ships that served as inspiration for the pioneers of modern architecture.

Photographs: Juha Ilonen

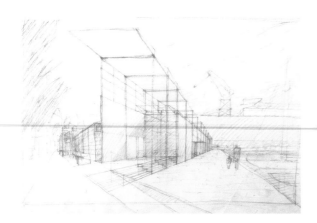

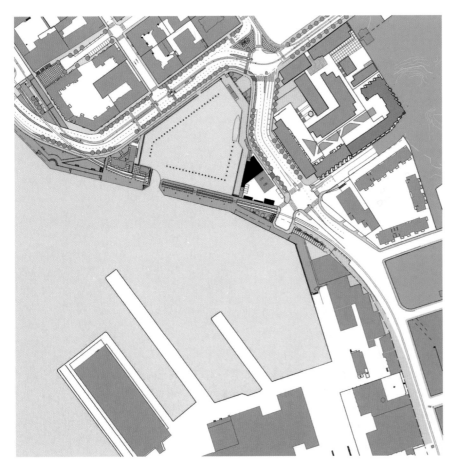

The soaring galvanized steel structure deliberately imitates the nearby industrial cranes and buildings. An elongated shape was chosen for two reasons: to ensure that all guests seated inside would enjoy views of the harbor, and as a visual reference to the passenger ships which are constructed near here.

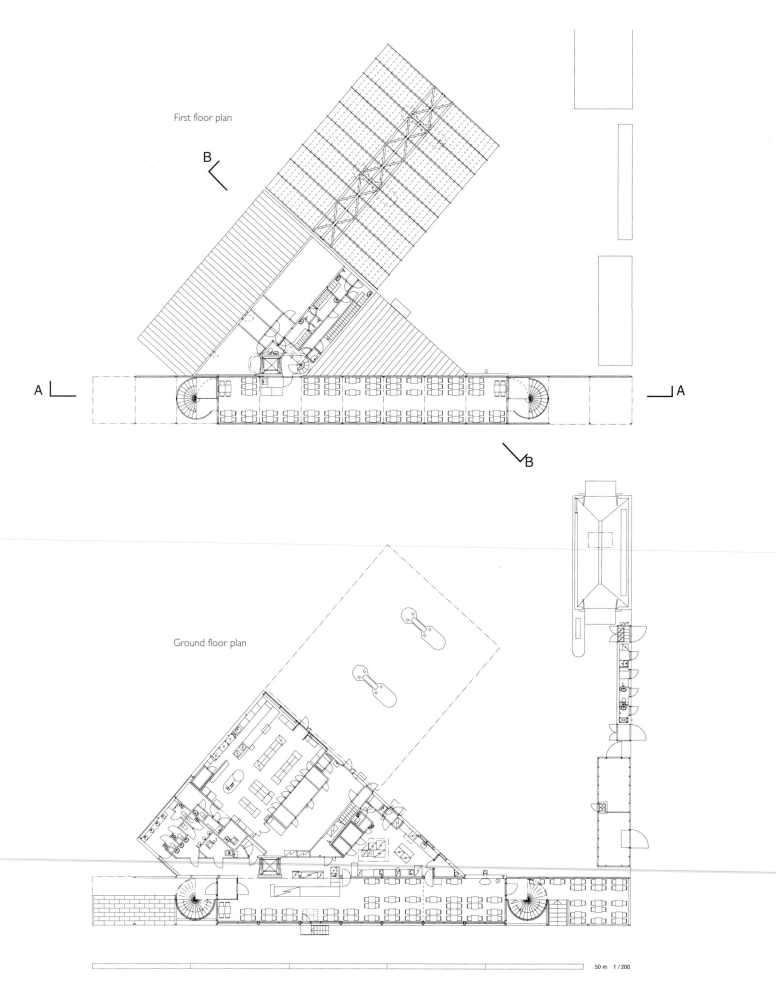

First floor plan

B

A

B

A

Ground floor plan

50 m   1 / 200

230

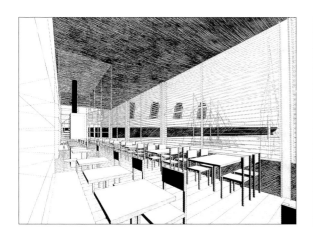

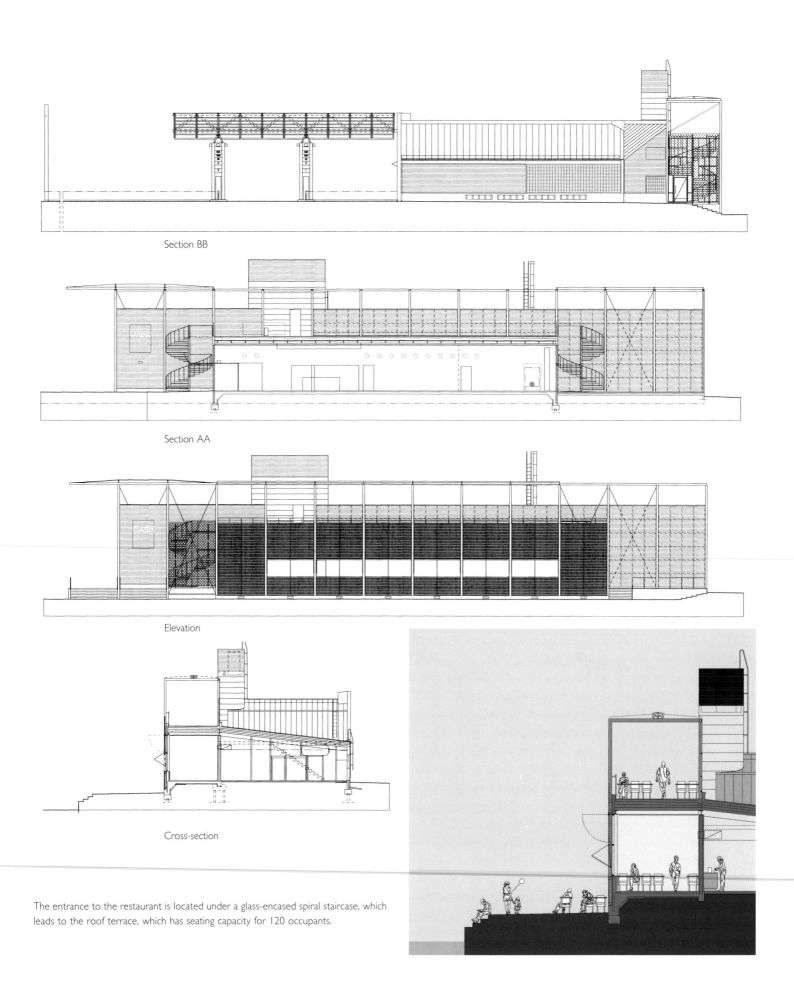

Section BB

Section AA

Elevation

Cross-section

The entrance to the restaurant is located under a glass-encased spiral staircase, which leads to the roof terrace, which has seating capacity for 120 occupants.

Jakob+MacFarlane
Restaurant at the Centre Pompidou

Paris, France

The program for this 900 m², top-floor restaurant had to somehow adapt to the pre-existing, highly individualized framework of the Centre Pompidou, itself a Parisian architectural icon. In view of this, the architects opted for creating a background presence of sorts, a non-designed, non-architectural response which would not interfere with the existing building. The end result is one large continuous space, which follows a basic grid pattern, broken up at one end by large irregular volumes.

Brushed aluminum, with tiles that follow the 80x80 pattern which regulates the entire building, was chosen for the floor for its qualities of alternately absorbing and reflecting light. The desired effect of achieving a subtly changing landscape between exterior and interior was thereby achieved with the lightest of touches.

Massive floor-to-ceiling "bubbles" clad in 4 mm-thick aluminum plates delimit the dining area at one end and create a surreal landscape, like dining amidst giant moon rocks. These volumes also serve the practical purpose of cloaking the kitchen, bar, coat check and private reception room.

These independently functioning volumes each receive their water, heating, ventilation and electrical supplies from above, on the roof.

Opposite this "moonscape" is a spacious 450 m² terrace. The interior space here seems to flow seamlessly into the exterior via a completely glazed wall with aluminum sashes.

Photographs: Nicolas Borel + Archipress

235

237

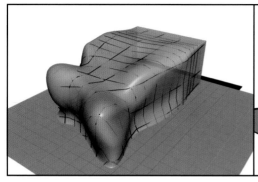
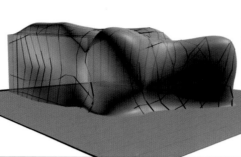
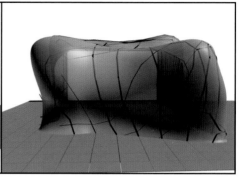

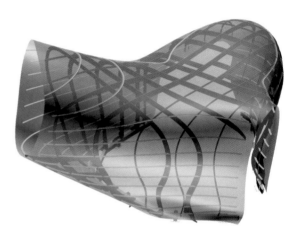

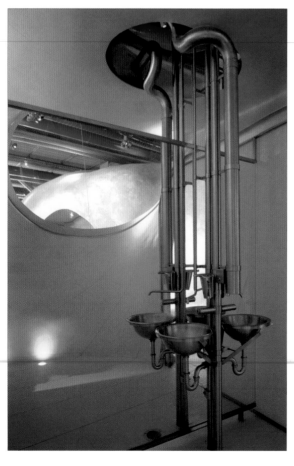

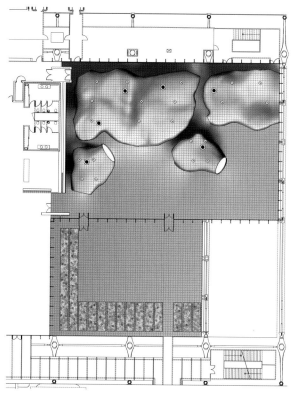

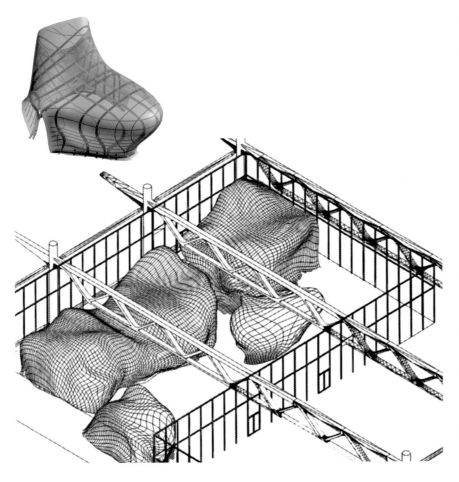

Javier Bárcena & Luis Zufiaur
Kiosk in Judimendi Park

Vitoria-Gasteiz, Spain

This project was for a small coffee-stand in Judimendi de Vitoria-Gasteiz Park, located on the east side of the city, at the end of Olaguibel Street. With a view to respecting the landscape and creating a magical place, the architects have designed a glass pavilion, which lies embedded into the natural surroundings. The cafe, like a refuge opening out toward the park, sits at the level of the garden, at the same height as the lawn and its surroundings.

A layer of transparent, screen-printed glass encloses the entirety of the program, which is grouped together on a single floor and surrounded by a partially-covered terrace. The interior partitions were done with sheets of cardboard and plaster over a core structure of galvanized steel. In the rooms which would be exposed to humidity, the kitchen and toilets, 15mm thick sheets of moisture resistant material were installed.

The absence of differing levels and hierarchies makes a stroll around the place easy, as one becomes familiar with architectural elements designed for leisure. The entrance is on the west side, next to an existing tree. Services such as the bar, kitchen, storage room and toilets were placed on the north face. Finally, the south face is the enclosed public space, while the covered terrace is just outside.

The architects used screen-printed glass as a chameleon-like skin which mimics the natural surroundings, seeking integration into the park, as opposed to camouflage.

The construction is based on a system of two slabs: one in the reinforced concrete floor and the other in the steel roof. This configuration, interwoven with a number of metal pillars, creates a completely transparent, glass system of "intervals", which open out to a panoramic view of the surroundings.

Thus, while the reinforced concrete floor slab rests on the ground like a carpet, serving as foundation and protecting the roots of the trees; while that of the roof is its opposite - whimsical, built with dry construction and housing a great deal of the installations.

Photographs: César San Millán

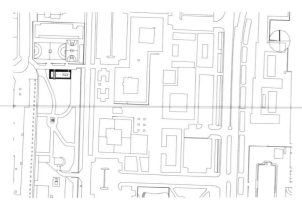

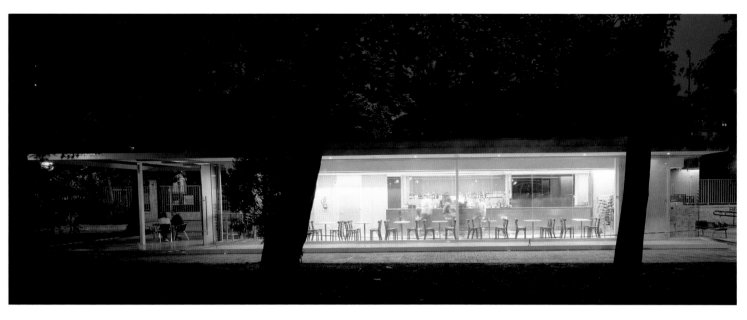

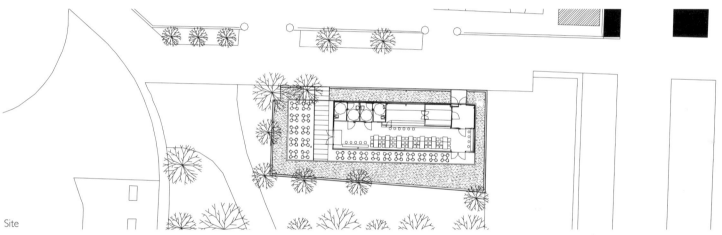

Site

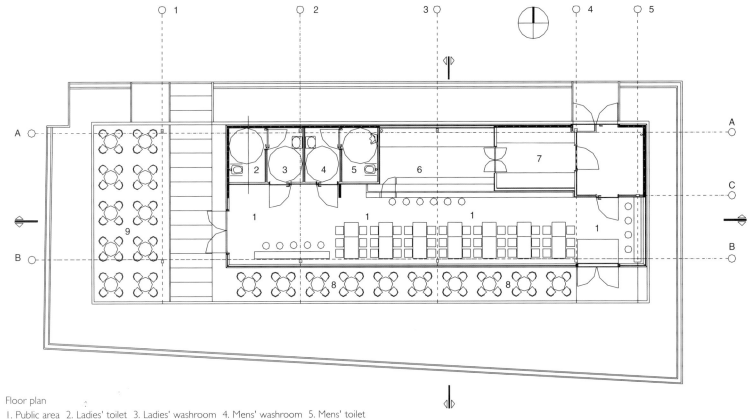

Floor plan
1. Public area 2. Ladies' toilet 3. Ladies' washroom 4. Mens' washroom 5. Mens' toilet
6. Bar 7. Kitchen 8. Covered terrace 9. Open terrace

West elevation

East elevation

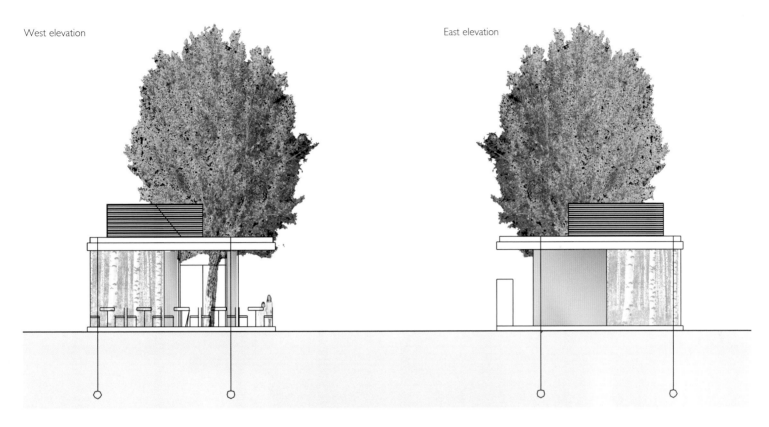

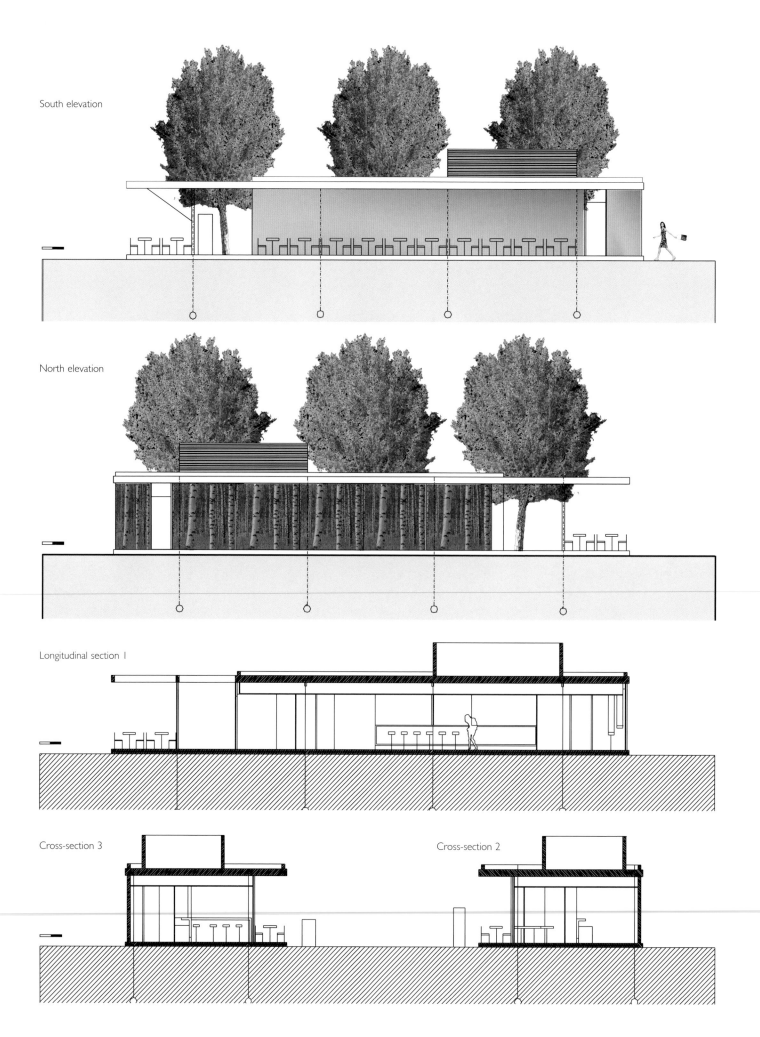

South elevation

North elevation

Longitudinal section 1

Cross-section 3

Cross-section 2

Giovanni D'Ambrosio
NERO Restaurant

Kuta-Bali, Indonesia

A low-tech approach, experimenting with light and vegetation as part of the design, was taken in the program for this restaurant in Kuta, on the island of Bali.

At noon, sunlight streams in through two narrow skylights running the length of the ceiling in the main room. Plants wind their way down sections of tennis net draped from the ceiling. In the evening, it is the subtle, modified lighting which gives color to the place, in harmonious collaboration with religious objects such as the Balinese altars dedicated to various spirits, which immediately acquaint us with the Balinese Hindu culture. While all materials are local, they have been "translated" into a modern style. The batù pilah stones, palm wood and small black river stones have been left in their original state, while the cement cubes and rectangles used for a part of the wall are the result of a type of local craftsmanship. The black ceiling is composed of the type of net which is normally used as solar protection in orchid nurseries. One of the walls is made from thousands of small wooden cubes, cut in different sizes, creating a rich depth.

The omnipresent Balinese rice paddies, whose watery surfaces reflect the passing clouds, were the inspiration for the use of mirrors here. The kitchen is contained within a huge cube covered in mirrors. This reflecting block creates the illusion of a deeper, wider space while also increasing the sensation of light. The tables chairs and accessories were especially designed for this project. The legs of the table pass through the tabletop, ending in arms which can hold flowers, candles or even bowls of fruit.

A small stairway cuts straight through the kitchen-cube and leads to the first floor. Here, guests dine while enjoying partial views through the semi-transparent curtains of plants.

Photographs: Cristopher John Leggett

More than a mere decorative element, vegetation has been incorporated here as part of the design. This, along with the use of local stone and palm wood, forms part of an intentionally low-tech architectural approach.

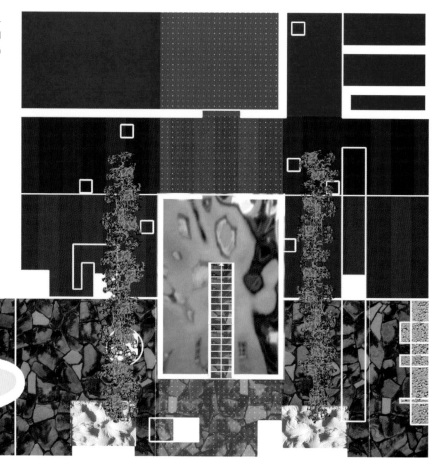

At night, soft lighting sets a romantic tone. By day, the same space enjoys a fresher ambience due to the natural light coming through two long rectangular skylights. The use of tennis net as curtains covered in plants is an ingenious reworking of an inexpensive, everyday material.

Thomas Schlesser
Blackbird Restaurant

Chicago, USA

Located on a strip of notoriously chic restaurants and bars, the design for Blackbird had to rise to the challenge of tough competition in order to make its presence known. Taking the "Less is more" approach, the clients requested an understated, streamlined look.

The building chosen for the project was a two-story brick building which had fallen into a state of neglect. The first step was to break open the brick "box" and to glaze the entire facade of the first floor, while translucent white plastic partially obfuscates the windows of the second-floor private dining area.

The interior was designed as "a box inside a box": the U-shaped banquettes on the second floor and the oak-lined bar on the first floor have been conceived as architectonic elements contained within the enclosure.

A feeling of openness and confident simplicity prevails. Perimeter lighting running the entire length of the wall makes the detached ceiling appear to float.

A narrow, enclosed stairway brings patrons to the middle of the second floor, where they are greeted by a custom-designed bar of stainless steel with an acrylic, under-lit surface. This floor has been set aside for private dining and cocktail receptions, with room for up to 100 guests. The ambience, while emulating the same pared-down feel of the main dining room, is more intimate. Here, gray carpeting absorbs sound and envelops guests, as opposed to the polished oak floors downstairs.

Photographs: Bob Briske & Reid Fogelson

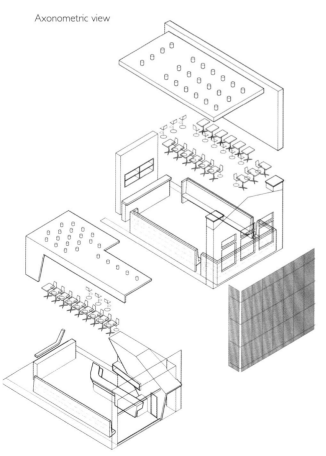

Axonometric view

257

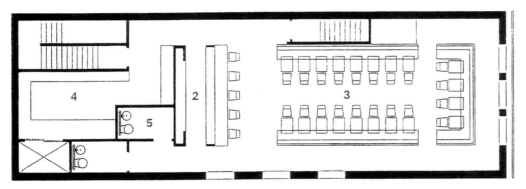

First floor plan

1. Entry
2. Bar
3. Dining room
4. Kitchen
5. Rest rooms
6. Elevator

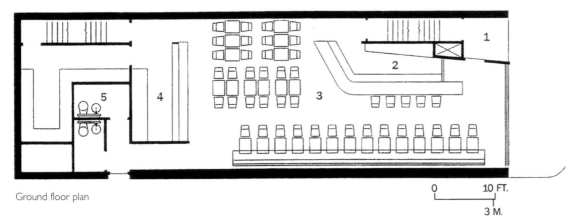

Ground floor plan

0   10 FT.

3 M.

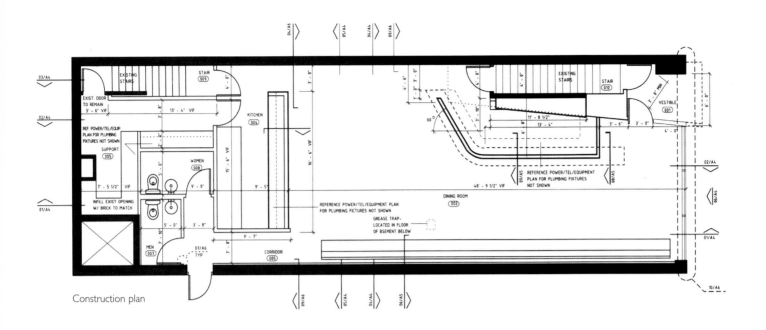

Construction plan

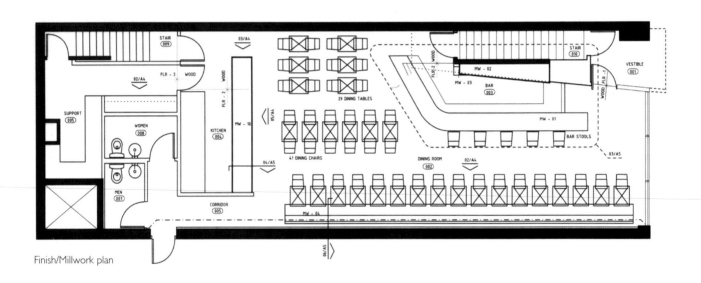

Finish/Millwork plan

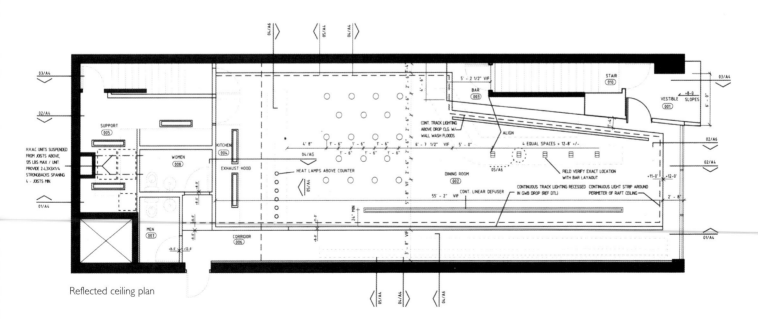

Reflected ceiling plan

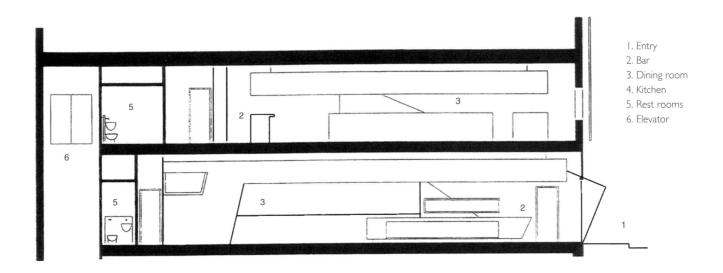

1. Entry
2. Bar
3. Dining room
4. Kitchen
5. Rest rooms
6. Elevator

Different seating arrangements on the ground floor

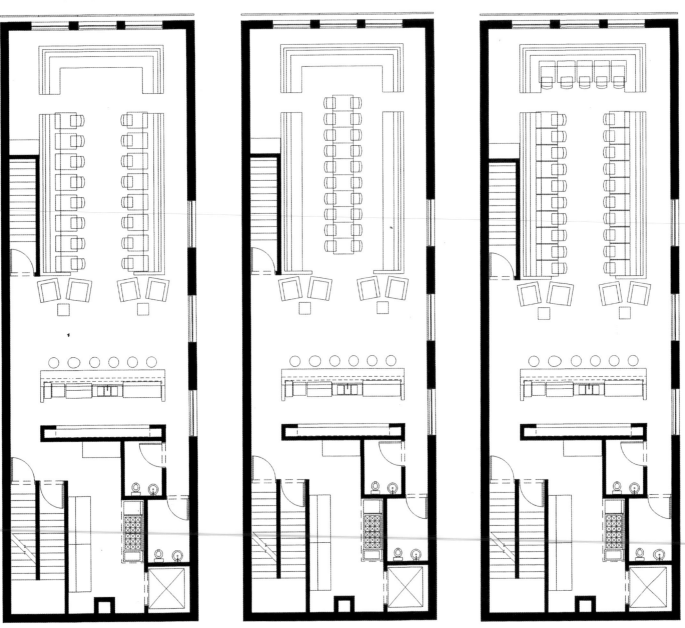

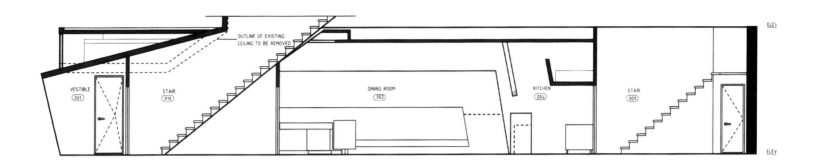

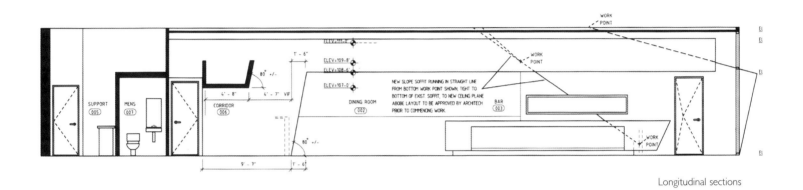

NEW SLOPE SOFFIT RUNNING IN STRAIGHT LINE
FROM BOTTOM WORK POINT SHOWN, TIGHT TO
BOTTOM OF EXIST SOFFIT, TO NEW CEILING PLANE
ABOBE LAYOUT TO BE APPROVED BY ARCHITECH
PRIOR TO COMMENCING WORK.

Longitudinal sections

BOX Architectes
TATU Bar + Grill

Belfast, Northern Ireland

The front elevation of this bar and grill is made up of a large projecting zinc canopy, which hovers above the second-story timber decked terrace. The glass facade -punched through by a zinc box- is partially masked by a large iroko screen which contains the signage.

The impact of the impressive height -9 meters- of the main space is maximized by a tight entrance. A heavy walnut ceiling, with a 1-meter perimetral light slot, floats overhead like a cloud. To one side, a dark walnut-panelled wall is punctuated by stainless steel and features custom-designed sandblasted lighting. The other side of this space is dominated by a 21-meter-long cast in-situ concrete bar, which begins at the front door and continues into the rear lower bar area, stitching the two spaces together.

The end wall is covered in 75 stainless steel pegs protruding 50 mm from the wall in a 750 mm grid. The texture of this wall changes constantly as light from the edge of the walnut "cloud" changes direction throughout the day, casting varying shadows from the stainless steel pegs.

Under the textured end wall, patrons drop down into the rear area into a much lower space. Here, the rear wall has been removed and replaced with a wall of translucent Reglit glass, which allows natural light to pour in during the day and is replaced by external lighting at night.

The restaurant area is defined by a curved alcantara wall. It has a very loungy feel and is equipped with cream carpet, leather sofas and walnut tables.

Photographs: Todd Watson

Floor plan

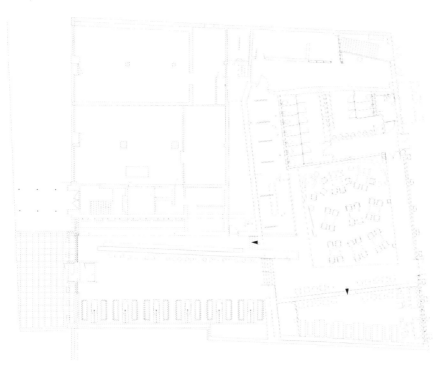

The dark walnut panelled wall is perforated by ventilation slots. The lighting is stainless steel and sand-blasted glass. The walnut and alcantara benches are bathed in natural light during the day via a glazed perimeter slot near the ceiling.

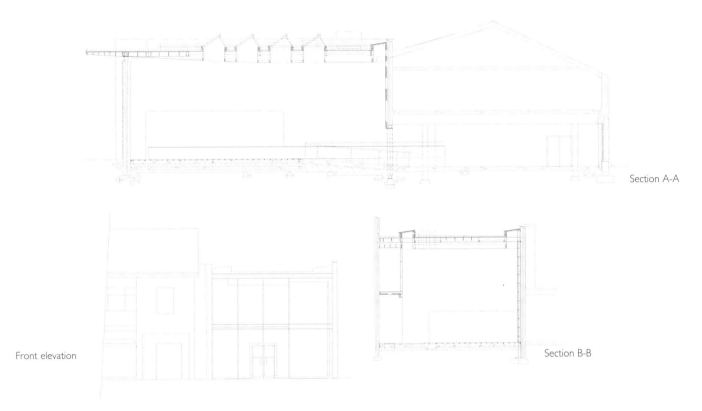

Section A-A

Front elevation

Section B-B

Claesson, Koivisto & Rune
One Happy Cloud

Stockholm, Sweden

Light and simple interiors have long been a Japanese tradition. Meditative and spatial calmness express the Japanese mentality. The three architects of this restaurant discovered that this philosophy was also close to Scandinavian tradition.

The One Happy Cloud restaurant was not intended to be yet another sushi bar. The food is intended to be "well-prepared, plain Japanese-Swedish fusion food".

The architects emphasized verticality and horizontality in the design. Two intersecting main axes were created. One of them lies parallel with the street, and the other goes straight through the building. The bar and the tables follow the axes.

Two long fluorescent light fittings complete the composition. The long wall behind the bar cuts through the whole restaurant and is painted with real blackboard paint. The artwork for the opening, made with white chalk, was done by graphic artist Nille Svensson, and is intended to be wiped out and replaced with new chalk-art every two months.

The Japanese references in the restaurant are subtle, so much so that the style of the restaurant is just as much modern Scandinavian as it is international. The colors are white, blackboard paint, concrete and oiled beech wood. Large acid-etched glass sheets (larger than possible in standard production) are used as space dividers.

The NXT chair was designed by Peter Karpf of i-form, Sweden, in oiled beech. The tables, benches, bar, beer taps and shelves were designed by Claesson Koivisto Rune, in oiled beech and galvanized steel.

Photographs: Patrick Engquist

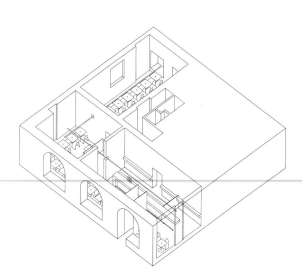

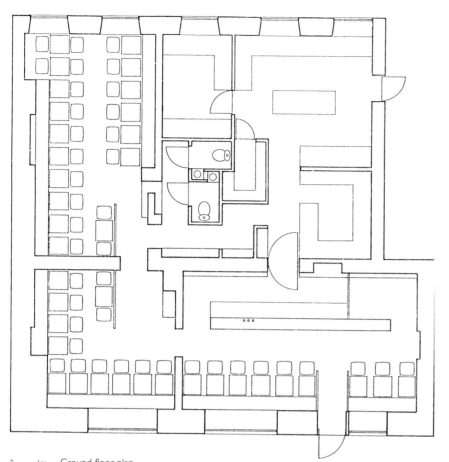

0   1m   Ground floor plan

272

A detailed view of the three stainless steel beer taps. These represent one of the few vertical elements which break up the marked horizontality of the whole.

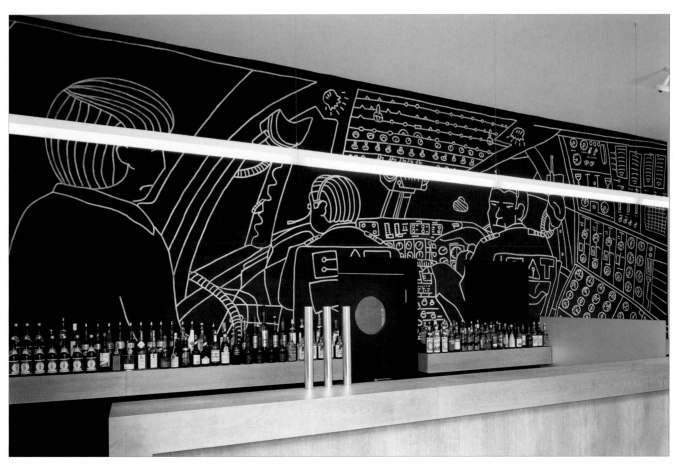

L. Paillard & A.F. Jumeau
Périphériques, architectes
Nouveau Casino

Paris, France

A 500 m2 nightclub filled with ever-shifting sights and sounds has been situated behind an early 20th century Parisian café.

Within the urban context in which the scheme is located, this music venue can reach a sound level of 135 dB. It is fully equipped with the technical facilities of a top-quality night club. Conserving the image and the environment of the Café Charbón, which is now a restaurant, the new casino has been created with a contemporary vocation, following to a certain extent the aesthetics of Star Trek.

The hall of the Nouveau Casino is like a deep cave with rough steel-covered walls in which one finds a very long bar of illuminated translucent resin with charming organic forms. Two staircases lead to a mezzanine, at the end of which there is a black bench that offers a wide view of the hall.

The frame of the roof was replaced by a new metal structure of S-shape profile placed on a mobile support between the first layer of thermal insulation applied to the original wall and a cavity filled with mineral wool. Poles of 9 to 15m were used to join it to the ground and to fit a floor on springs. On this floor slab a Mégastil porticoed structure was placed, supporting the second thermal layer (stucco + vegetable wool + tarpaulin) and totally separated from the side walls. It is "a box within a box". This structure contains all the technical facilities of the hall: ventilation, air conditioning, electrical circuits and lighting.

All these systems are concealed behind the inner metal ceiling of the box, which is made of triangular panels joined to a series of steel porticoes that fully occupy the free space. These panels form a roof on the fragmented surface and are made of absorbing and reflecting steel plate. The triangles conceal six video projectors that cast images and numeric videos that are multiplied by mirrors, accompanying the concerts and exhibitions and illuminating the walls of the hall. The image cast is the final layer of the ceiling: a motif in movement, like a "paper screen".

Photographs: Luc Boegly / Archipress

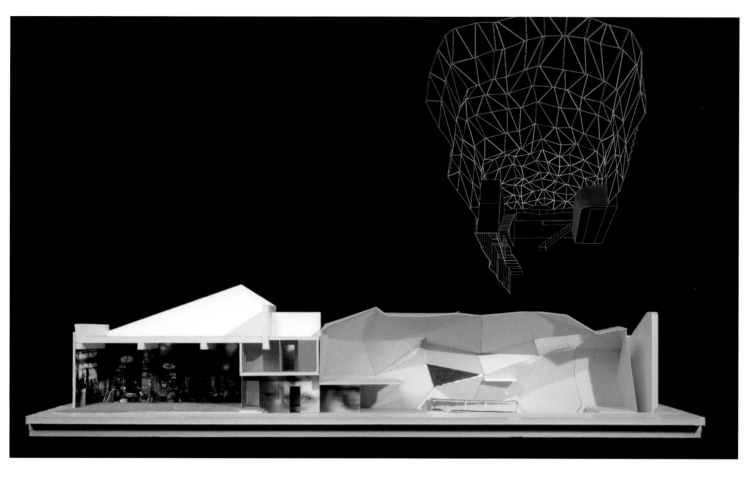

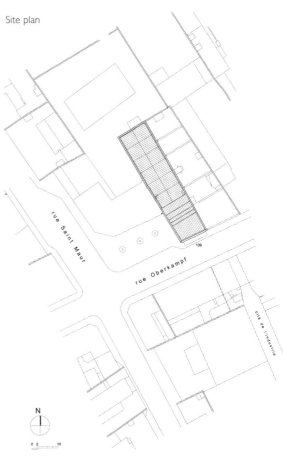

The classic image of the Café Charbon, now converted into a restaurant, contrasts with the modern look of the Noveau Casino. Here, the lighting and slide projections interact with the irregularity of the walls and ceilings in order to create a unique atmosphere.

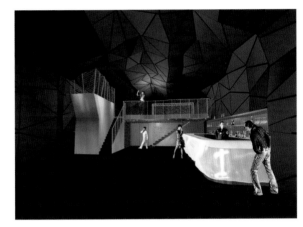

Floor plan

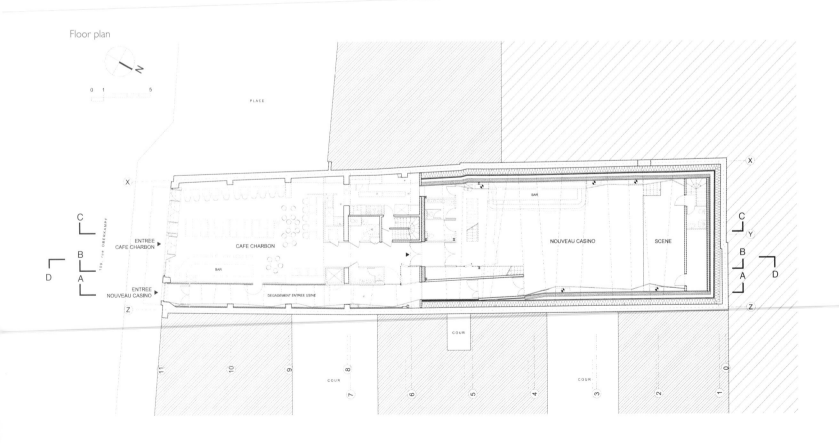

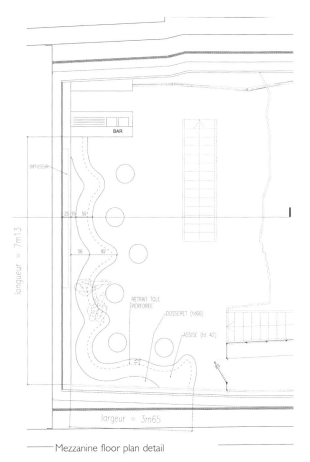

Mezzanine floor plan detail

Mezzanine floor plan

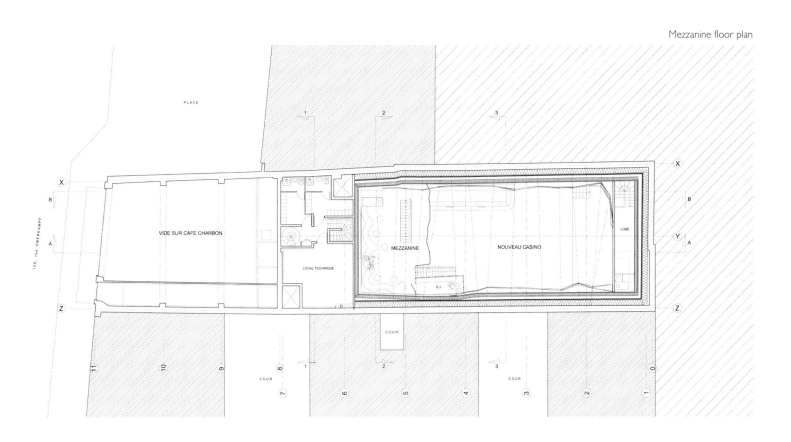

The ceiling panels are done in sheet-metal and conceal a sophisticated system of lighting and video projectors. This system allows the ambience to be changed at will to fit the desired mood.

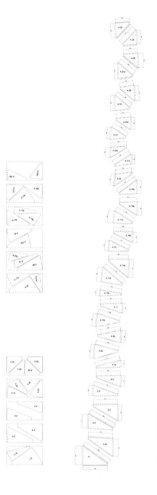

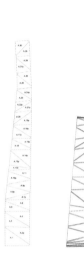

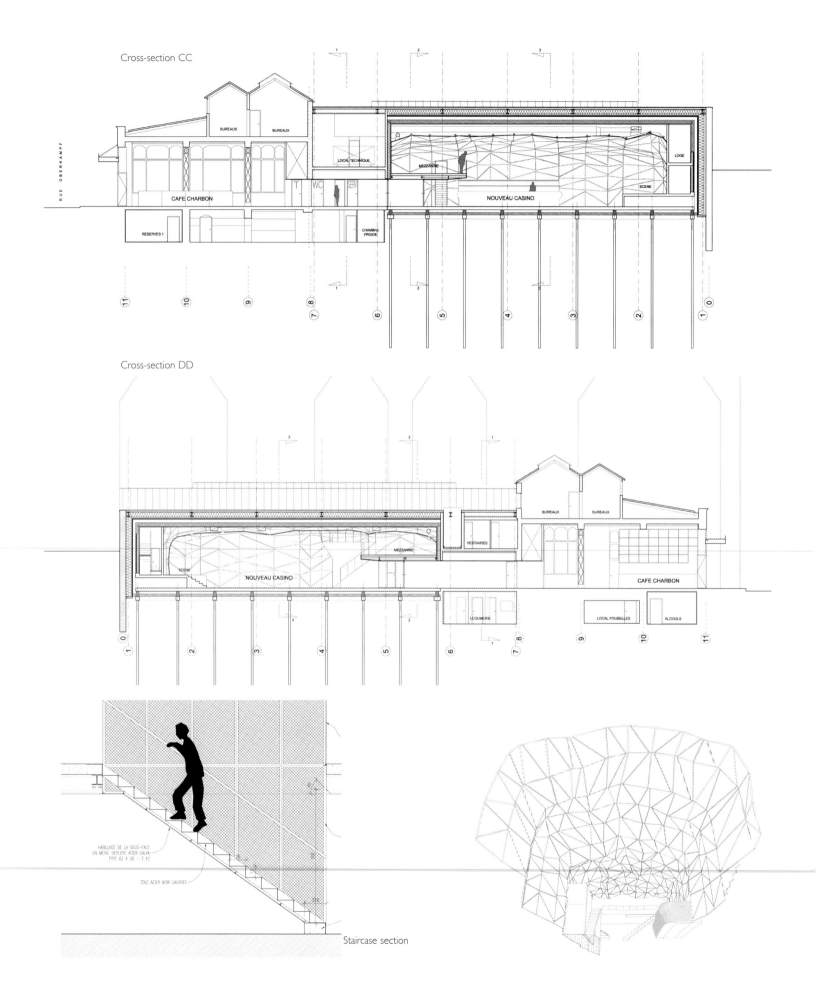

Cross-section CC

RUE OBERKAMPF

BUREAUX   BUREAUX

LOCAL TECHNIQUE

MEZZANINE

LOGE

CAFE CHARBON

T   WC   SERV

NOUVEAU CASINO

SCENE

RESERVES 1

CHAMBRE FROIDE

11 10 9 7 8 6 5 4 3 2 1 0

Cross-section DD

BUREAUX   BUREAUX

VESTIAIRES

MEZZANINE

SCENE

NOUVEAU CASINO

CAFE CHARBON

LEGUMERIE

LOCAL POUBELLES   ALCOOLS

1 0 2 3 4 5 6 7 8 9 10 11

HABILLAGE DE LA SOUS-FACE
EN METAL DEPLOYE ACIER GALVA-
TYPE 62 X 30 - 3 X2

TOLE ACIER NOIR GAUFREE

Staircase section

282

Cross-section AA

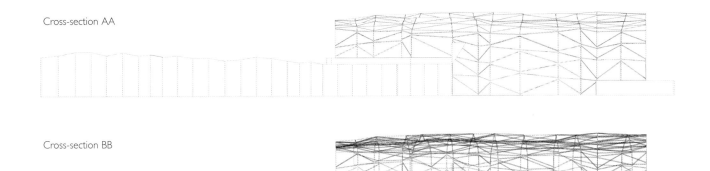

Cross-section BB

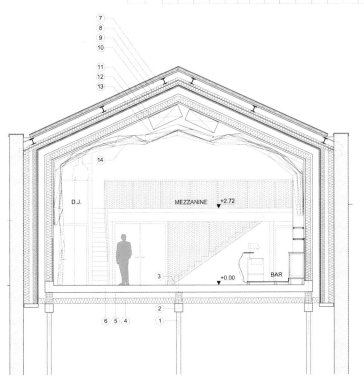

Cross-section
1. d=15 cm
2. Brace
3. Spring
4. 20 cm insulating material
5. Air chamber
6. Concrete slab
7. Steel casing + 10 cm vegetable wool
8. Metal structure
9. 20 cm vegetable wool
10. BA13 + Viscoelastic + BA18 over a Megalist shell
11. 20 cm vegetable wool
12. 2xBA13 + BA18 over a Megalist shell
13. Metal porticoes
14. Roof of crude steel
15. Existing party walls

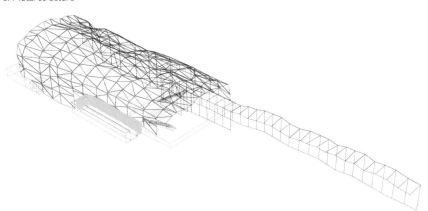

Thom Mayne - Morphosis
Lutèce Restaurant

Las Vegas, USA

The noise and chaos that reigns in Las Vegas' casinos is no accident - it is part of a carefully thought-out plan. By the same token, the serene ambience of this elegant restaurant is a direct result of the architects' plan of creating a haven from the pervasive din of the gambling floors.

The central architectural element, from which the rest of the spaces are structured, is a smooth elliptical form which wraps around the dining area. In the entryway, patrons find themselves in front of the gently-curving outer wall of this form. They are guided past a floor-to-ceiling, glass-encased wine rack, which holds 5000 bottles, and into the sophisticated, restrained central space, where a bar serves guests awaiting tables.

The black floor and ceiling pull away into the background, ceding importance to the bronze bands spiraling around the upper portion of clean white walls. A massive chandelier with exposed spotlights and bronze strips, presides over the dining room, tilted at an odd angle. Unpredictable, non-uniform curves interrupted by sharp geometric shapes overhead create a constant sense of motion in the dining area.

The anchoring element in this scheme is the art piece which is set into the floor, just under a one-inch-thick sheet of laminated glass. This piece, by artist Do-Ho Suh, is comprised of 19,000 PVC human figures placed by hand in a translucent polyurethane resin base. With arms raised above their heads, these figures support the glass of the floor.

Photographs: Farshid Assassi & Brandon Welling

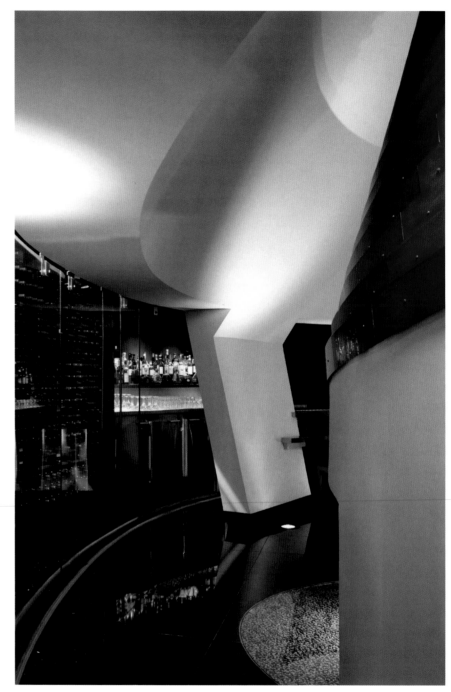

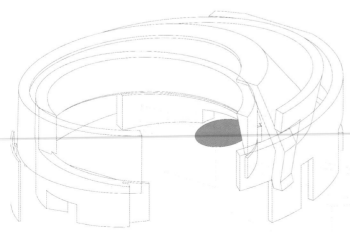

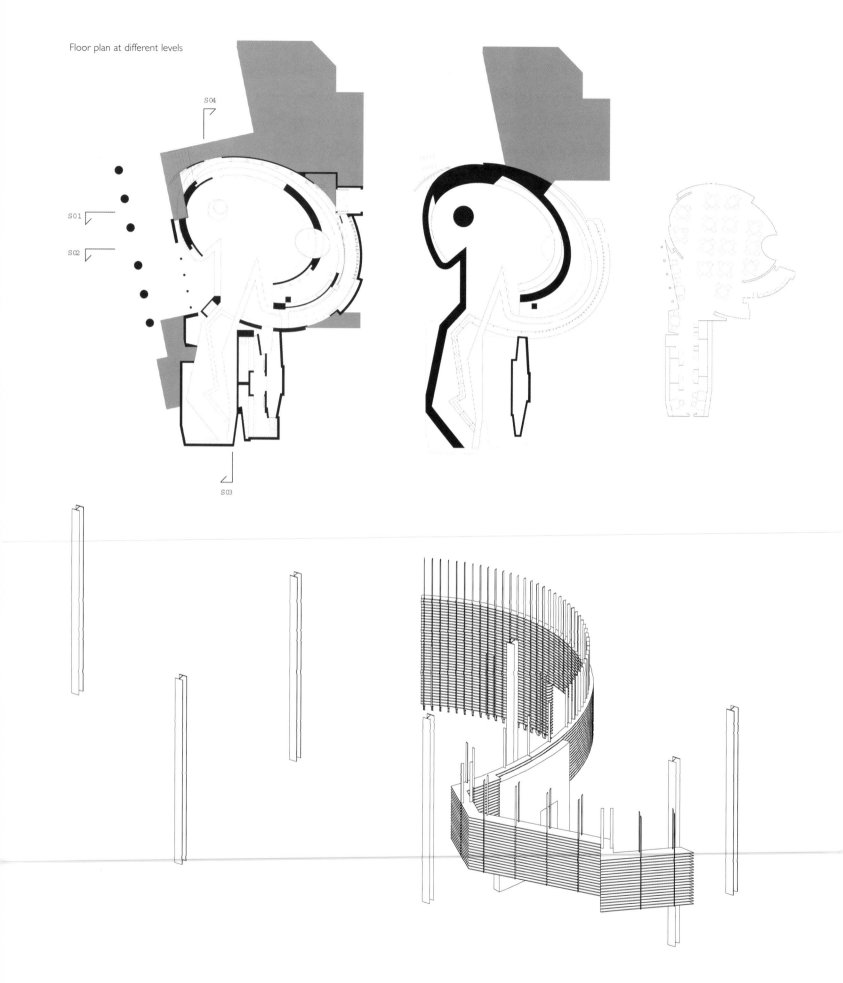

Floor plan at different levels

S04

S01

S02

S03

286

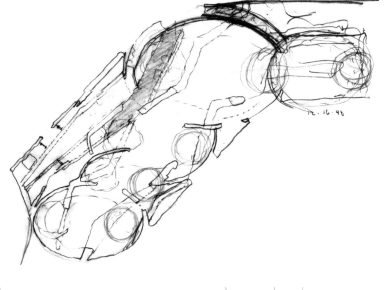

Cross-section C

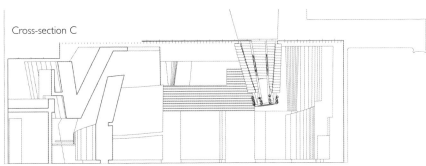

Cross-section D

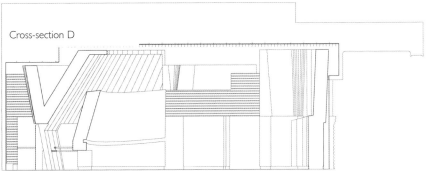

Cross-section B

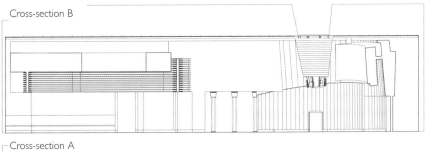

Cross-section A

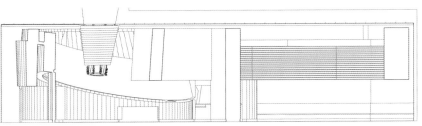

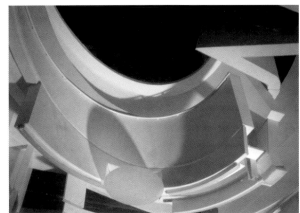

Michael Young
Bar Astro

Reykjavik, Iceland

There are literally only a handful of buildings in Reykjavik which are around 100 years old. So even though this refurbished dance club (with four bars and two dance floors) was located in a building which was only 90 years old, it is protected by law as a historic structure. "There was not a straight line anywhere, so my first task was to sort out the geometry," says the architect.

The program drew extensively on Icelandic craftsmanship for inspiration. Local builders are especially skilled in concrete, steel and stone work, which is widely used in geothermal pools in Iceland. The design is a cross between a dry, indoor swimming pool and a picnic area concept, built with the assistance of a local company which had done work on a nearby geothermal pool. Since Iceland is usually very cold and windy, the idea was to bring a bit of the outdoors inside, livening it up and adding warmth with liberal splashes of color.

The furniture surrounding the central pool was custom-designed by Sawaya & Moroni and Cappellini. The architect created a number of woven steel lights to assist with the artificial nature aspect. The atmosphere is surreal, like stepping into computer animation; Corian was used on the bar surfaces and shelves, intensifying that look.

Upstairs, where there is an ambient floor and the private, members-only Red Room, a more relaxed atmosphere prevails. Thermo-formed walls in the Red Room contain a lighting system that reacts to movement. When guests are sitting and talking, the walls are a pale pink; as people start to move and dance the tone deepens gradually to red.

Photographs: Ari Magg

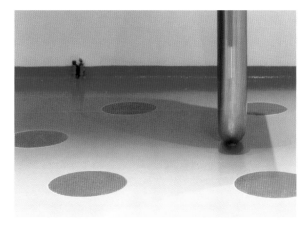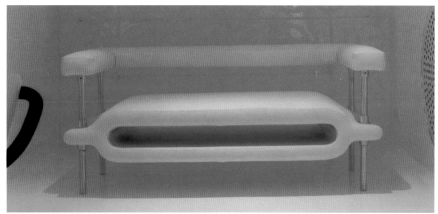

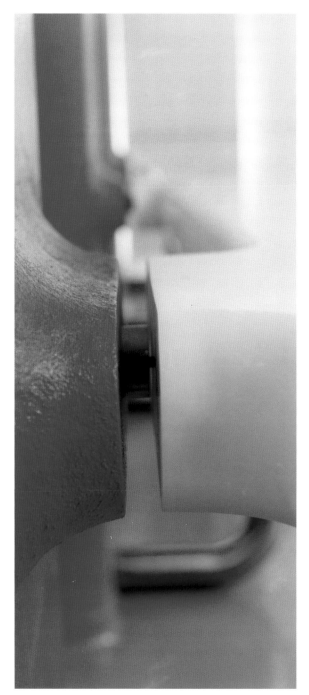

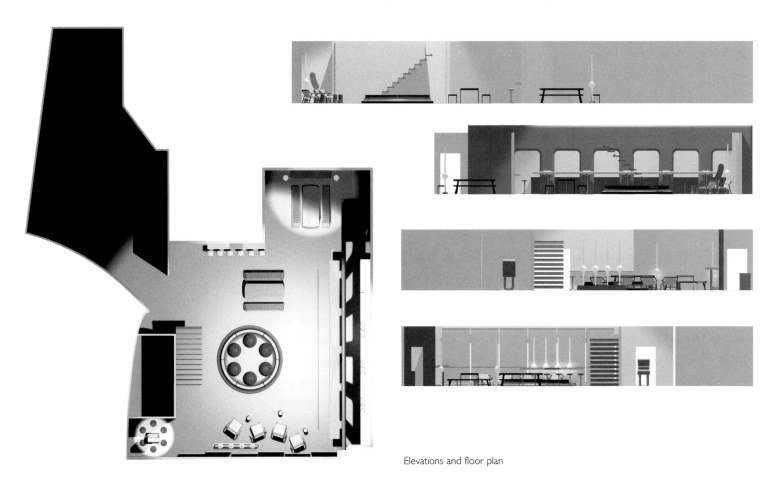

Elevations and floor plan

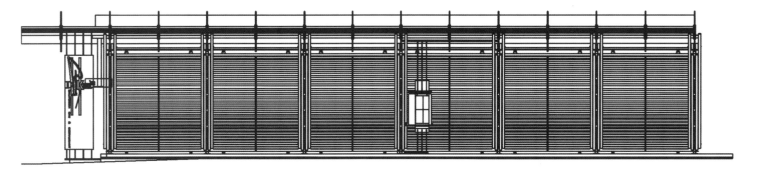

Facade elevation

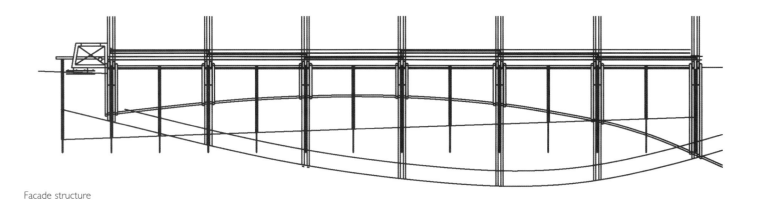

Facade structure

The load-bearing steel structure and sheet-metal roofing were retained from the original building. The new spatial demands caused by the creation of a new stairwell were resolved by a separating wall in reinforced concrete, behind which are located the toilets and service areas.

Cross-section A

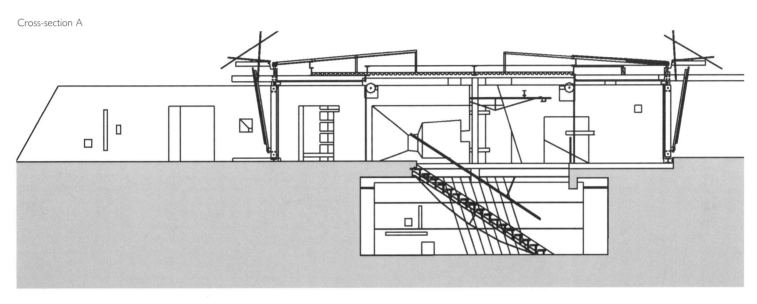

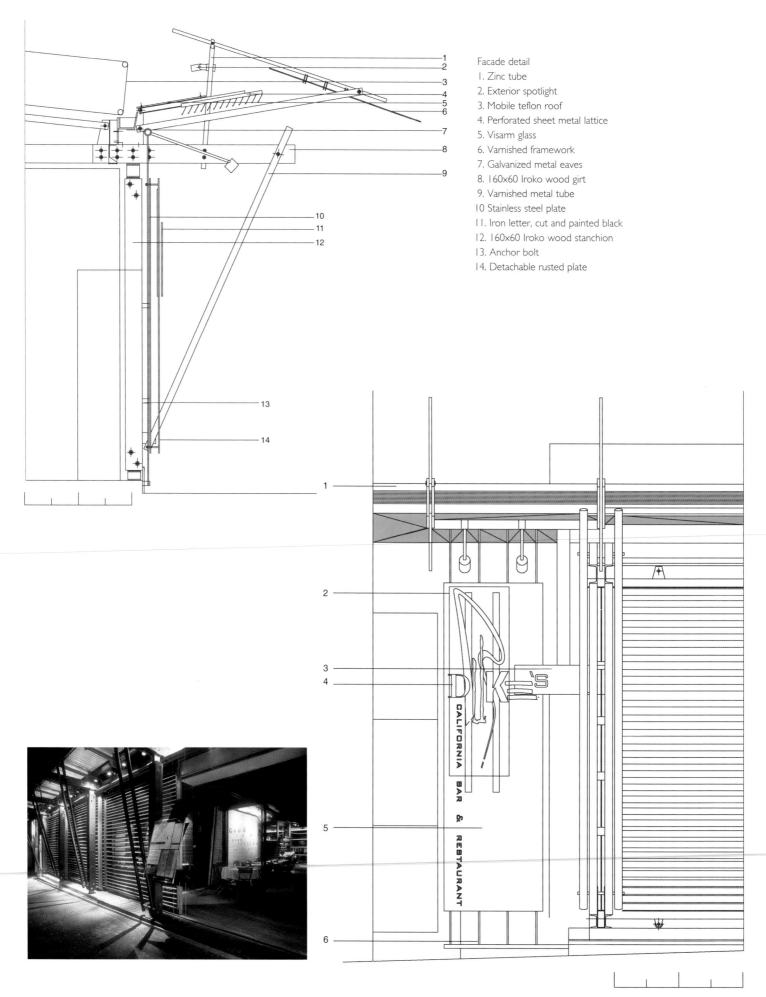

Facade detail
1. Zinc tube
2. Exterior spotlight
3. Mobile teflon roof
4. Perforated sheet metal lattice
5. Visarm glass
6. Varnished framework
7. Galvanized metal eaves
8. 160x60 Iroko wood girt
9. Varnished metal tube
10 Stainless steel plate
11. Iron letter, cut and painted black
12. 160x60 Iroko wood stanchion
13. Anchor bolt
14. Detachable rusted plate

The wooden slats adorning the ceiling are meant to evoke the planks of a California seaside boardwalk; and, also in keeping with the project's theme, the shape of the bar imitates a wave.

Javier García-Solera Vera
Dock and Services Building in the Port of Alicante

Alicante, Spain

In this scheme the architects took the opportunity to design the docks of the port of Alicante as part of the public space, so that it could perform its function but also be enjoyed for itself. Following the guidelines of the brief, a small building was placed on the dock as an approximation to the precision and quality of the materials of the shipbuilding industry. Built with dry joints of wood and metal that are assembled, fitted and bolted, this structure serves as a bar and as a sign of hope for passengers setting sail from this port.

An asymmetrical dock was thus proposed that looks in a specific direction in order to prevent the boats from obstructing the views from the building.

A minimum height was used in order to respect the horizontal nature of the port views, and it offers a clear verticality to greet those arriving in the city, in competition with the masts of the sailing boats moored in the harbour.

The limits have been clearly dissolved, and the architecture explores the margins and border territories. The exterior is merged with the interior and aims to achieve a new vision of the sea, a more intimate relationship that allows it to be enjoyed and shared. To achieve this, its proximity is reinforced by the overhang of the building, by the transparency under the wooden boarding and by the total absence of railings. The interplay of planes defining the architecture is organized so as to protect the premises from the noise of the nearby road and to allow the gentle changes in the sound of the sea to be heard.

Ultimately, the scheme shows its concern for clarity and transparency, merging with its environment and seeking complicity with the users. The building is not imposed upon the surroundings but is rather a silent, yet suggestive, presence.

Photographs: Duccio Malagamba

South elevation

North elevation

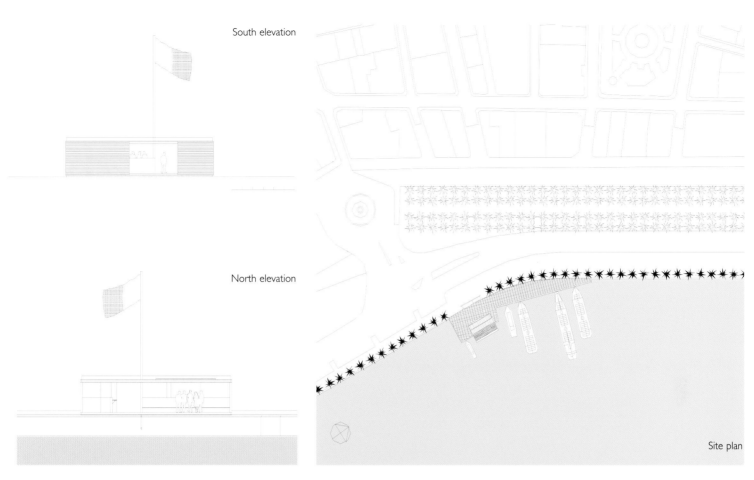

Site plan

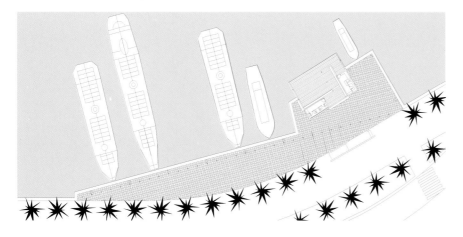

To accentuate the connection between the bar and the sea, it was decided that the terrace should overhang the dock and that the dock should be free of railings to avoid visual barriers.

Site plan

Elevation

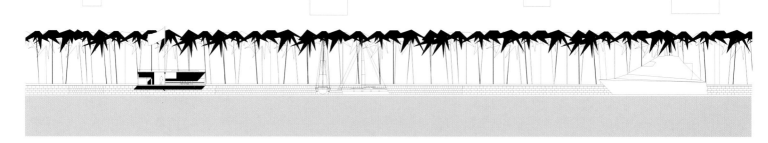

The interior of the bar is simple and elegant. Both the materials used and the construction system are similar to those used in shipbuilding, thus ensuring quality and long life for the building.

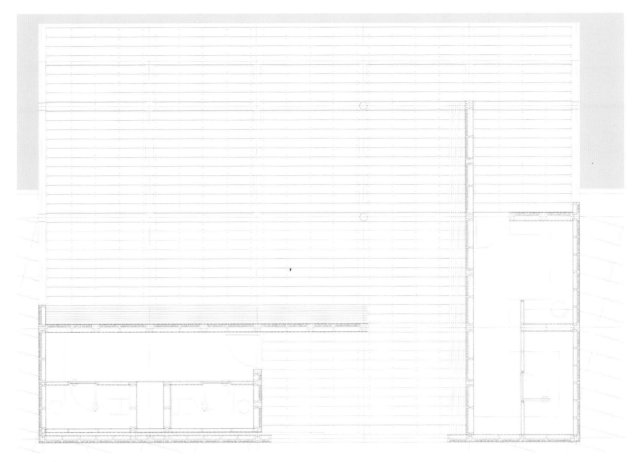

Floor plan

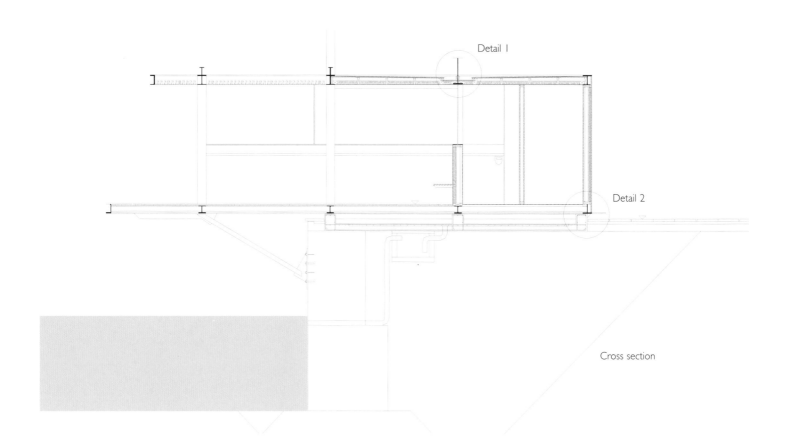

Detail 1

Detail 2

Cross section

Detail 1

1. 12 mm Okumen plywood board
2. Neutral sikaflex silicon glazing
3. Tubular profile painted 80.30.2 mm painted steel
4. 1.550 mm painted steel profile
5. Plywood with 15 mm phenol finish
6. Polyester gutter done in situ
7. Neutral sikaflex silicon glazing
8. 5+5mm safety glass

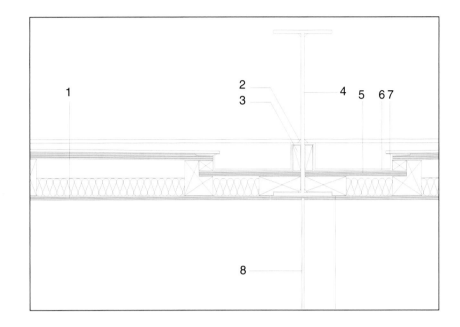

Detail 2

1. 19mm Eyong phenol plywood board
2. 100.50.3 mm painted steel tubular profile
3. Wood batten
4. 60 mm thermal insulation
5. Phenol board and aluminum slat
6. Painted steel H200 profile
7. Wood casing
8. Neutral Sikaflex silicon glazing
9. 40mm natural stone floor
10. Bond coat
11. 15cm reinforced ground slab

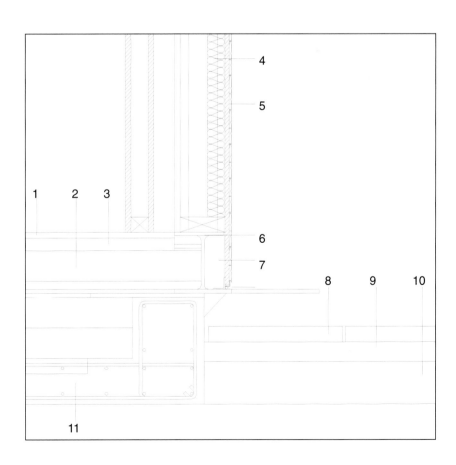

Dunlop Architects Inc.
Point Edward Charity Casino

Ontario, Canada

The program for this casino made use of the framework of an existing rail freight building located just steps from an old ship-loading dock. The unobstructed roof structure, with intricate trusses at 12 and 6-foot intervals for the whole 700-foot length, provided the principal structure.

The existing building had several unique features, one of which was the series of concrete ramps used for loading and unloading ships' cargo. Today, one of these ramps was turned into an elongated external waterfall, crossed by a wooden bridge.

The most striking element is the building's new tower. Reminiscent of a ship's smokestack, this tower attracts attention during the day. At night, it becomes a remarkable "lighthouse", whose magical lighting beckons for miles.

Inside, the entire casino is built around a sea theme. All of the elements are designed to transport casino patrons from the surface of the sea in the lobby area, to an underwater environment in the gaming area itself.

In the lobby, a glass wall encases five large salt-water aquariums. Also, the base of the copper-clad tower continues into the interior of the building here, set above a sheet of water that dances with artificial and natural light.

On the promenade to the game floor area, one encounters three large waterfalls spilling over the top of a 16-foot-high concrete wall, then over a stainless steel ledge and dropping down a slate tile surface into a series of water channels below. Openings in this wall provide glimpses of the game floor.

In the gaming area, the other side of the waterfall wall is a 300-foot-long, 18-foot-high ship's hull. Cladding was created from cold rolled steel, evenly heated with a blow-torch to create large organic patterns of dark blue, purple and deep red on a silver surface. There are a series of ships' masts, randomly spaced and angled, supporting the theatrical lighting for the ceiling.

Photographs: Interiorimages. Ca

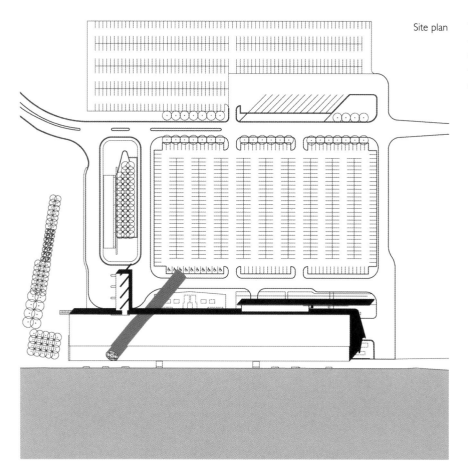

Site plan

The site's dual nautical/railway heritage is emphasized on the facades. The water side of the casino is open, fluid and colorful, with a copper-clad tower patterned after a ship's smokestack. On the land side, the building has a sleek enclosure, suggesting train cars. An aluminum "wave" softens the lines.

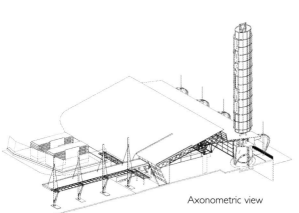

Axonometric view

Floor plan

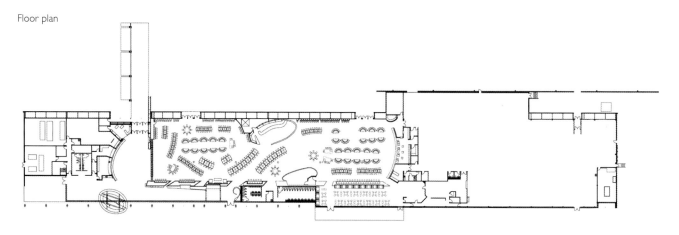

The detached ceiling in the bar is shaped like a massive (60 foot long) floating stingray, made of gunmetal colored space frame with triangular, translucent acrylic tiles. Computer controlled lights create the illusion that the stingray is swimming.

Below, the hull and ribs of a large boat have been suspended from the ceiling of the restaurant.

320

Architecture Studio
Cafétéria du Parlement Européen

Strasbourg, France

Located in one of the most emblematic buildings of Strasbourg, the European Parliament, this bar stands out at first sight because of the bold composition of its floor. In order to make this space something more than a simple place of consumption, the team of architects, Architecture Studio, decided to change the concept of the space completely through a simple but startling device: as if it were a field in spring, the bar shows photographs with vegetable motifs under its translucent floor. The color green thus dominates the whole surface, dotted with yellow, white and fuchsia flowers that reinforce the effect. This creates a peculiar atmosphere that is conducive to relaxation, and proposes an interesting reflection on our attitude towards nature. Another of the outstanding elements in the design is the curved metal bar that invites the customers to get closer, and stands out within the general linearity of the space. It occupies almost all of the ground space in the double height area, freeing it from being too close to the ceiling and standing out against the background of vegetation. Two slender beer taps are set into the bar counter.

Just opposite the bar there is a large glass door that fills the interior with daylight. A similar doorway provides access and the premises are closed with an elegant sliding wall. White curtains hang over these doors, creating a subtle angle, which curves gently and reflects the light from the skylight.

Photographs: G. Fessy & R. Rothan

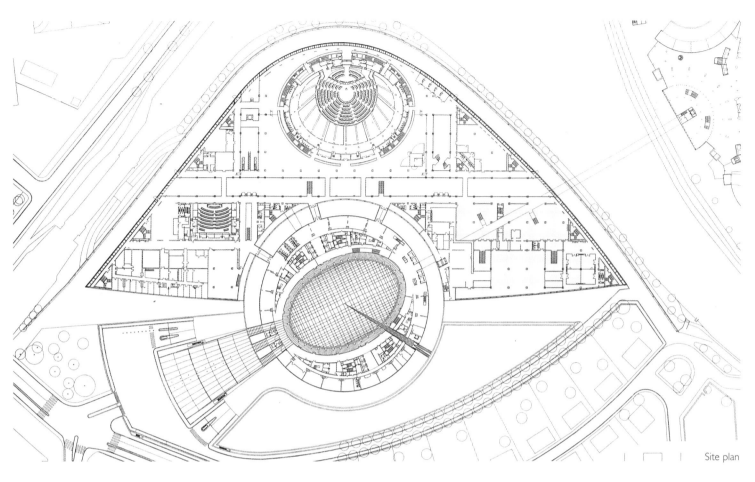

Site plan

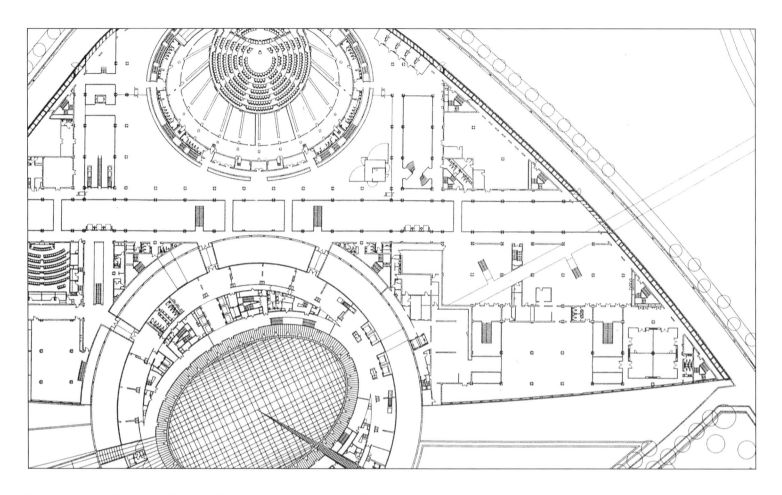

Besides being one of the most emblematic buildings in Strasbourg, the European Parliament has four different bars (journalists, members of parliament, visitors and general) that follow the same pattern.

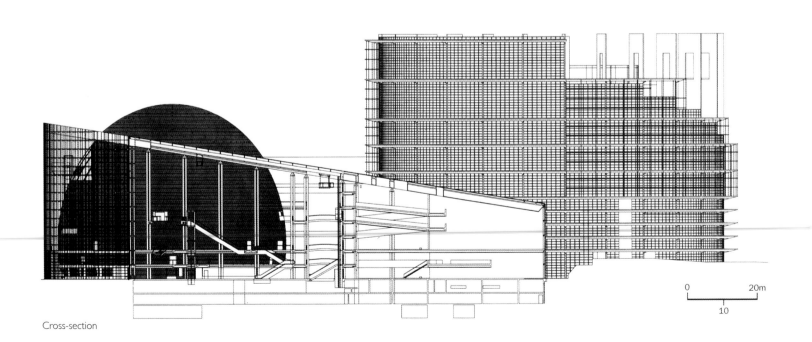

Cross-section

0   10   20m

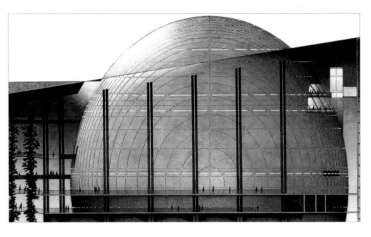

Ron Arad Associates
Belgo Central

London, UK

The "Belgian" Restaurant concept rehearsed in Chark Farm has now moved to the West End, this time with triple capacity, sidewalk café, beer store and offices. This project makes the glistening engine of the restaurant -the kitchen- into a spectacle of space, light, machinery and action that can be seen and heard not only from the street outside but from the farthest reaches of the restaurant.

The scheme inhabits a vast vaulted warehouse basement on a wedge-shaped site, bisected by a three-story entrance zone. By removing two of the vaults in a three-vault bay, the remaining vault creates a "bridge" between two new entrances. The bridge thus crosses a new vertical shaft of space perpendicular to a 60m-long avenue of columns crossing the restaurant below. The bridge is open on each side to the steaming kitchen below and offices above, while concealing miles of duct and pipe work within its belly. From the bridge, one descends to the restaurant in an industrial scissor elevator that is brightly back-lit so that the scissor mechanism, mesh cladding and entering customers make a slow-motion kinetic silhouette as it operates. At the restaurant level a glazed serving counter spans a third of the 60m avenues, separating the open kitchen space from customers and visually connecting two dining halls.

The long kitchen counter displays its huge stock of dishes and pots like an etched glass vitrine; this horizontal beam of light leads to the two vaulted dining halls where reflecting copper clad "pods" conceal dishwashing machines; in the beer hall, "hills" of rolled aluminum connect long benches and separate the backs of diners while the restaurant side has free-standing banquette "islands" for privacy seekers. London's first communal WC has been compacted into a free-standing serrated aluminum structure attended by a communal wash basin; finally each dinning hall has a 12 m-long bar dispensing Belgian brew from barrels visible behind sliding mesh panels.

Photographs: C. Kicherer

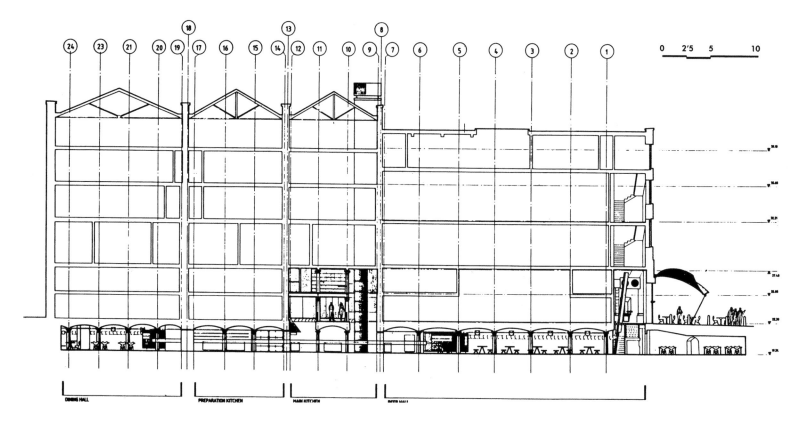

Longitudinal section through the restaurant

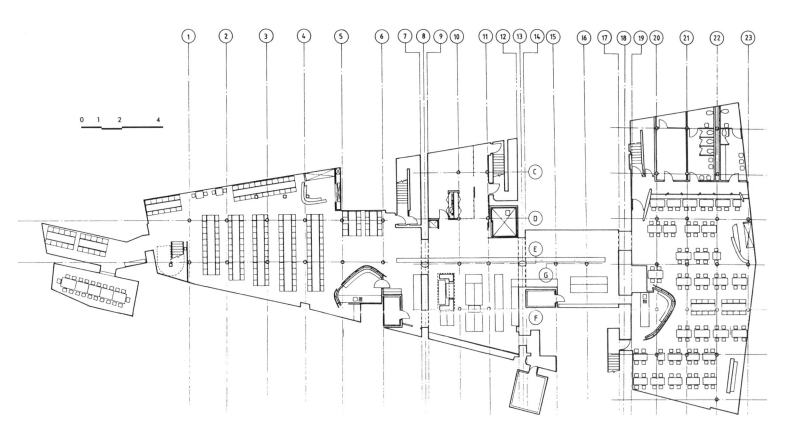

Lower level floor plan of the restaurant

Office dA
Mantra

Boston, Massachusetts. USA

Located in a space formerly occupied by the Old Colony Trust Bank, Mantra restaurant emerged out of two divergent architectural strategies. The existing space, although dilapidated and worn, was composed of tall proportions clad in an extravagantly grained marble and a steel-lined vault, replete with a monumental three-foot-thick vault door. A simple archeological approach of renovation and reconstruction is all that was needed in order to restore the space to its original aura and splendor. At the same time, the mandates of a restaurant would require spaces of varying kinds, some public, others more intimate.

The thematic transformation of the space -the importation of Indian silks, tents, jali screens, among other allusive techniques- are brought to the project to provide different dining and leisure environments while giving cultural specificity to the proposal.

The service spaces of the restaurant are lined by plush silk curtains, which serve the dual purpose of concealing the support areas from public view and acting as acoustic control devices. Polished plaster-lined volumes drape from the ceiling in three niches to conceal all mechanical spaces containing HVAC, sound and lighting elements. Tall metal chain-mail scrims line other public zones, partially concealing the private rooms. A glass screen frames the view of a back alley, a narrow urban trough of space delicately and surreally exposed to the lush dining interior. A laser-scored steel mirror ripples as a folded ribbon behind the length of the bar reflecting a distorted image of the space to its audience.

Of the various installations, one piece stands out as the restaurant's anchoring axis: a floor-to-ceiling structure of wooden slats known as the Hookah den. A monumental figure within the urban interior, the structure houses low couches as a space of repose for a more intimate ambience.

Photographs: John Horner

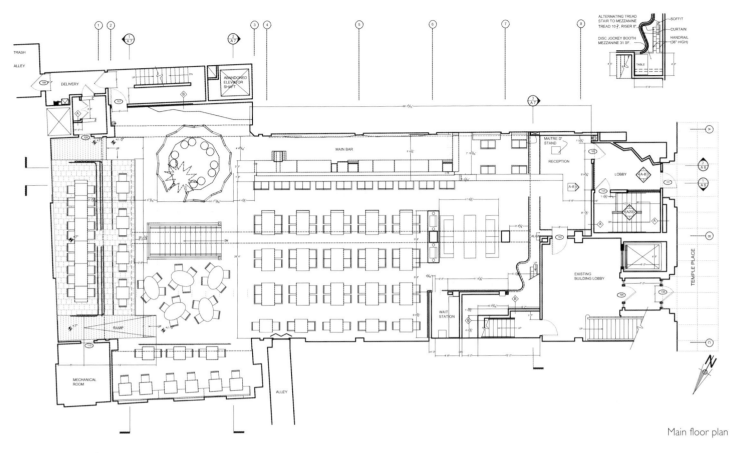

Main floor plan

Scketch of bar, mirror and Hookah Den

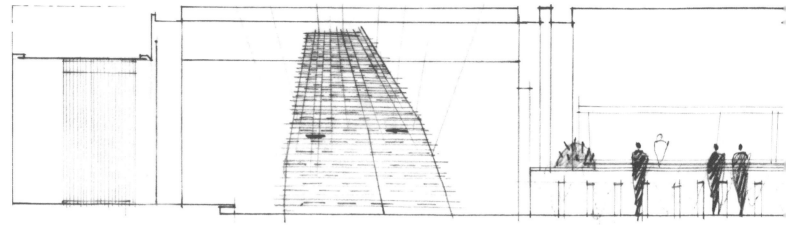

The evenly-spaced wooden slats of the hookah den -which is the central structuring axis of the restaurant- provide enticing glimpses of its dimly-lit interior.

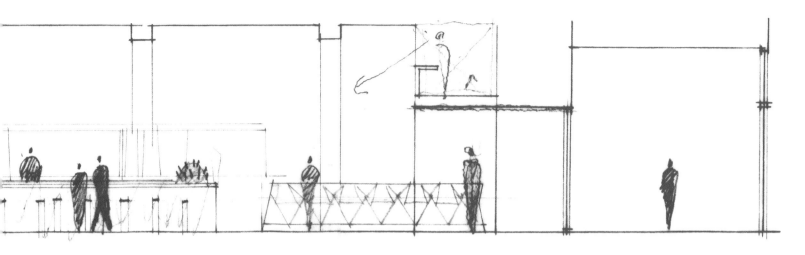

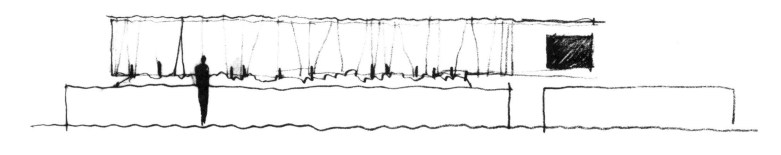

Scketch of Hookah Den

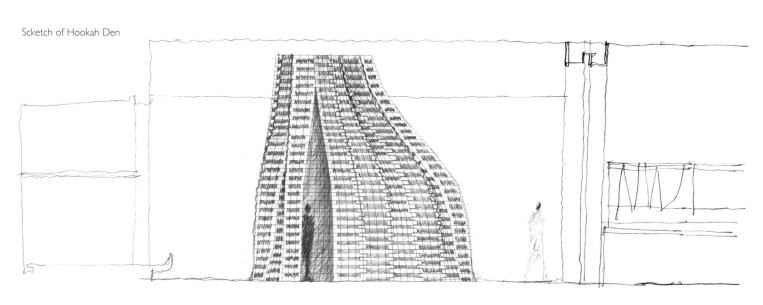

3D Model of Hookah Den   Plan view of Hookah Den

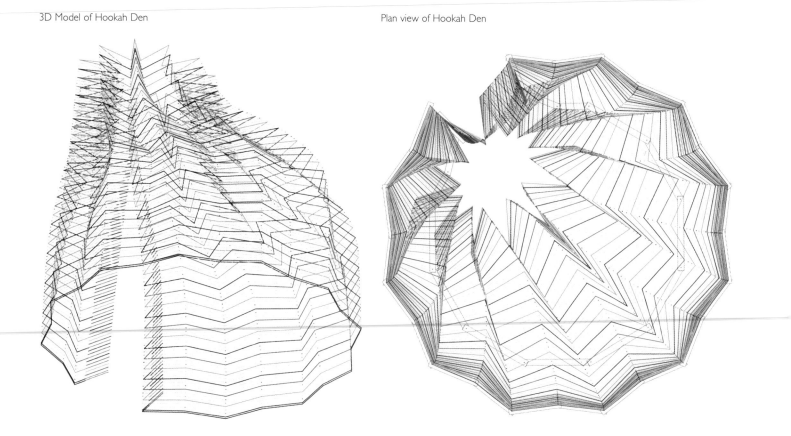

Steel, wood, plaster, glass and silk are some of the materials which come together here to form a coherent whole. The general layout of the entire space shows the sheer number of different created spaces and atmospheres.

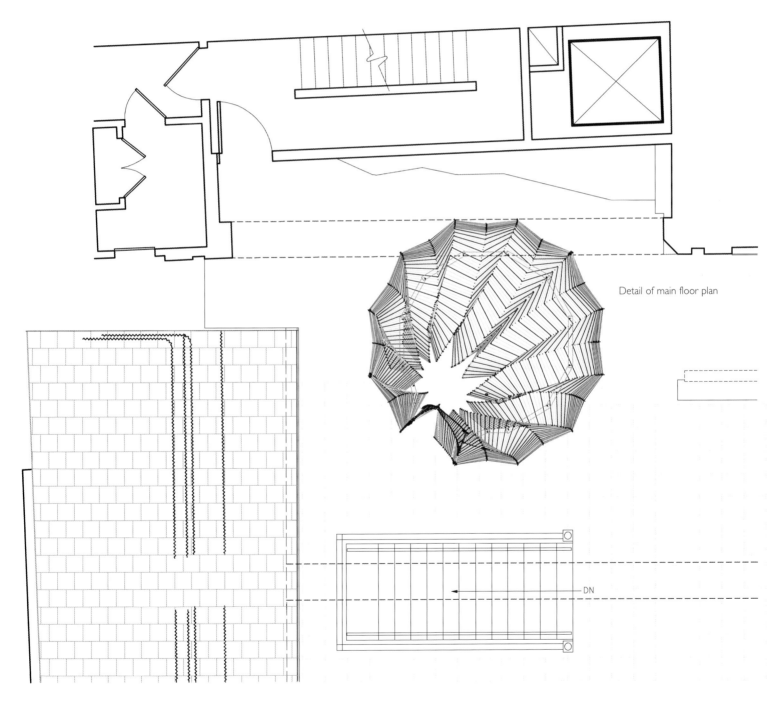

Detail of main floor plan

DN

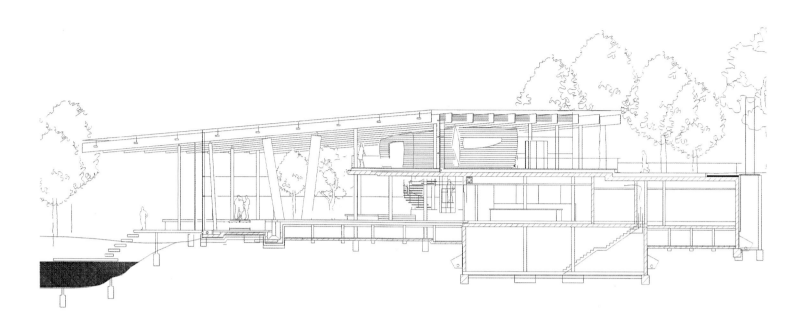

The supports for vertical load transmission continue the image of random tree trunks in the woods. The facade of steel and glass is inserted between roof level and floor surface, independent of the support structure.

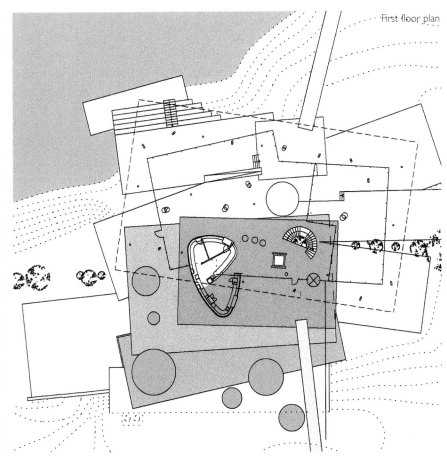

First floor plan

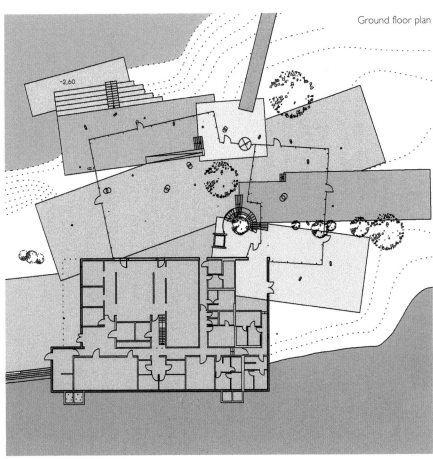

Ground floor plan

343

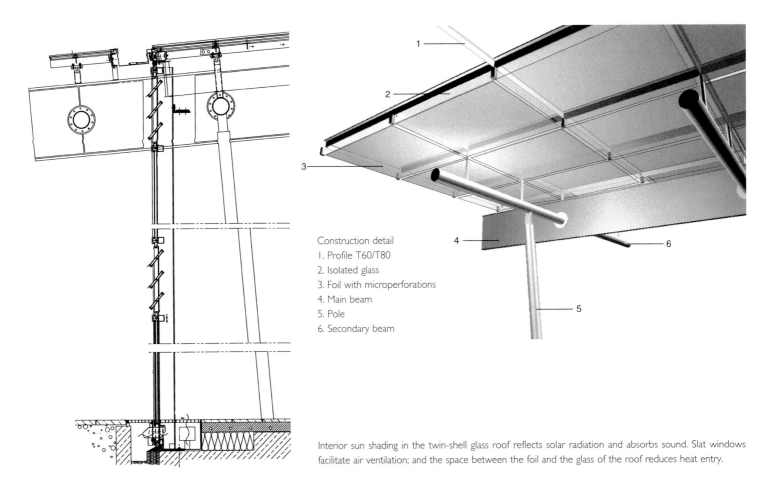

Construction detail
1. Profile T60/T80
2. Isolated glass
3. Foil with microperforations
4. Main beam
5. Pole
6. Secondary beam

Interior sun shading in the twin-shell glass roof reflects solar radiation and absorbs sound. Slat windows facilitate air ventilation; and the space between the foil and the glass of the roof reduces heat entry.

Marco & Gianluigi Giammetta
Reef Restaurant

Roma, Italy

Located in Rome's Piazza Augusto Imperatore, this recently refurbished restaurant specializes in fish. Hence, the fish and sea motif which is the driving force behind the program. Aside from the very literal interpretation of this theme seen in the enlarged silk-screen print of hundreds of gaping fish dominating one wall and the massive fish eye staring out from another print, most of the allusions are much more subtle and work together to create an overall impression of the sea.

Light reflecting off the floor makes it seem to shimmer like a watery surface, an impression created by the use of metal and sandwiched glass. Likewise, the ceiling is composed of suspended sheets of cracked glass, a technique which creates the illusion that the dining area is underwater. The selective use of metal mesh imitates the look of fishing nets; while a transparent pattern of deliberately rusted iron rods evokes the weave of ropes on a ship. In the main dining area, an elliptically-shaped wooden floor recalls the deck of a boat washed up onto a sandy beach. Even the color scheme -turquoise, light blue and green- is meant to evoke a sub-aquatic world.

The interior space of the existing building was originally two separate levels. However, the architects opted for sacrificing a great deal of the floor space on the upper level in order to create a majestic double-height space in the main dining area. The second level is now a balcony where diners enjoy a view of one entire continuous space.

Glass has been used in abundance not only to further the illusion of water, but also in order to maximize the light. A wall of translucent madras glass separates the kitchen from the dining room and the facade is almost entirely glazed.

Photographs: Luigi Filetici

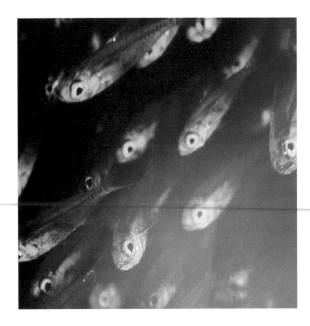

Most of the floor space on the second level was removed, leaving enough for balcony seating, in order to create a double-height space in the dining room. The glimmering, suspended ceiling panels are of cracked glass.

Ground floor plan

Underground floor plan

The colored lighting is another detail which is meant to create the sensation of being underwater. The floor is composed of sheets of metal and sandwiched glass, which imitates the affect of a shimmering surface of water. Translucent madras glass separates the kitchen from the dining room.

The fish motifs are silk-screened prints on forex. A portion of the dining area has been placed under the section of the second floor which was retained from the original structure. Thus, a different ambience has been created here, much more cozy and intimate than in the spacious main dining area.

Gehry Partners
Condé Nast Cafeteria

New York City, USA

Located on the fourth floor of the new Condé Nast Publishing Headquarters, this 260-seat cafeteria was intended to provide employees with a convenient lunchtime dining and meeting facility and includes a main dining area, a servery and four private dining rooms.

The main dining area is organized to provide a variety of seating arrangements in an atmosphere that is both intimate and open. Custom designed booths that accommodate 4-6 people each are distributed along the perimeter walls. These walls, which are clad in perforated blue titanium panels that include an acoustic backing to insure sound absorption, undulate in response to the geometry and overall configuration of the booths. Additional booths are located on a raised seating platform, which is enclosed within curved glass panels in the center of the main dining area, the floor of which is an ash-veneer plywood. The ceiling is clad in perforated blue titanium panels that match the perimeter walls.

The servery, which is adjacent to the main dining area, is a fully equipped facility that provides a selection of different hot and cold entrees. The servery's curvilinear stainless steel countertops, blue titanium walls and canopies, and ash veneer floor and ceiling compliment the sculptural and aesthetic character of the main dining area.

The four private dining rooms are located on the same level as the main dining area and the servery, but they are distinct and separate spaces to be used for special lunch meetings and presentations. The walls, floors and ceilings of the private dining rooms are ash-veneer plywood. Curved glass panels articulate the East wall of each room, providing an even natural light illumination through clerestory windows. The private dining rooms are equipped with state of the art audio/visual capabilities. Three of the four private dining rooms have movable partitions, allowing for a variety of spatial configurations to accommodate special occasions.

Photographs: Roger Dong & Condé Nast Publications

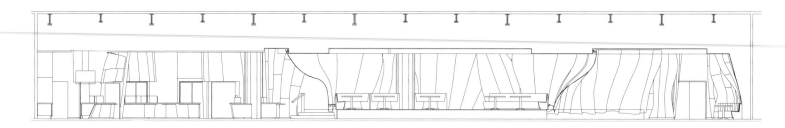

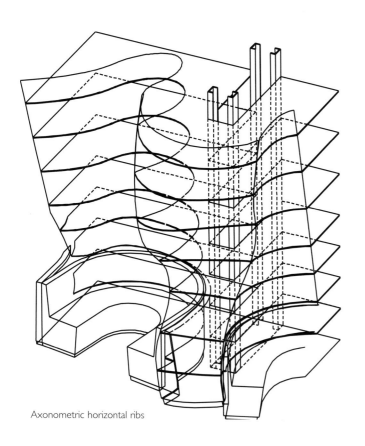

Axonometric horizontal ribs

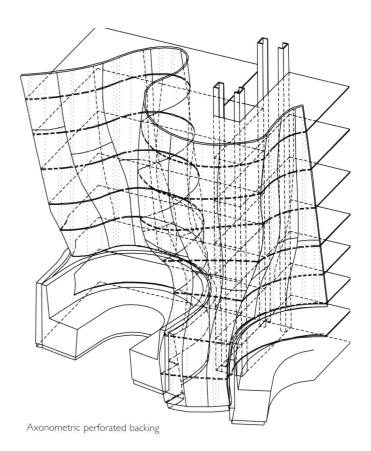

Axonometric perforated backing

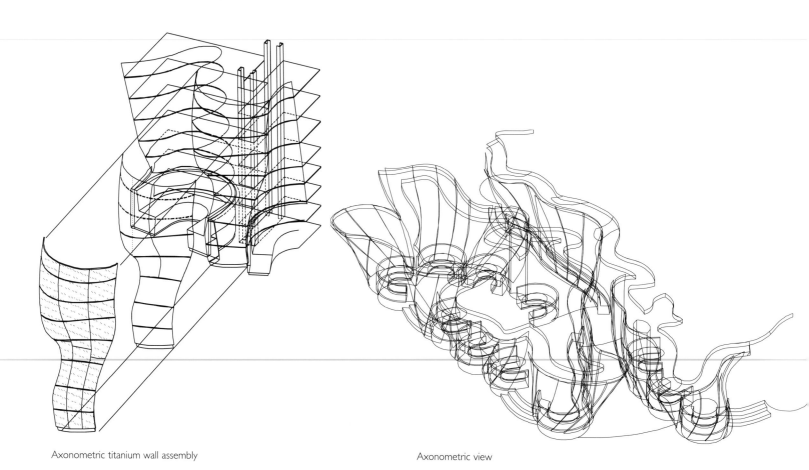

Axonometric titanium wall assembly

Axonometric view

356

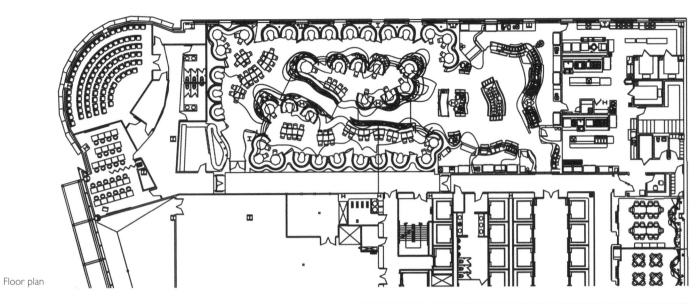

Floor plan

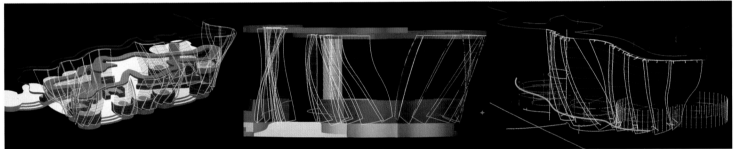

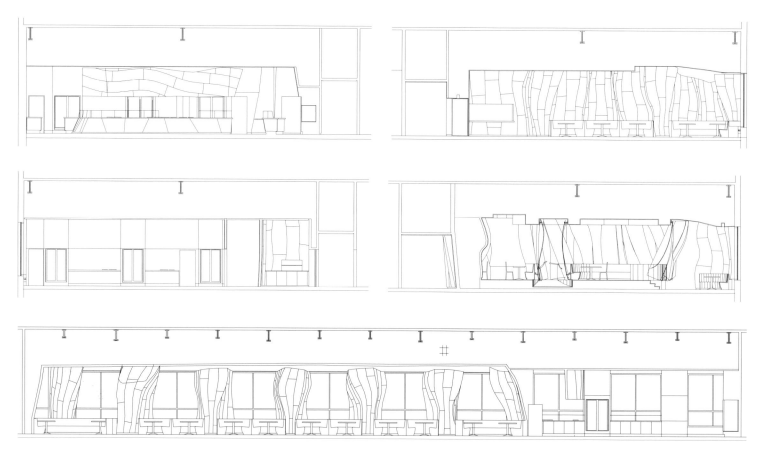

Sections